ClickStart
GUIDES

WORD 2013
TO THE
POINT

Quick solutions to all of
your Microsoft Word
questions

— comprehensive and to the point!

by **Scott DeLoach**

Microsoft Word 2013 to the Point
Scott DeLoach

Copyright © 2013 by Scott DeLoach

www.clickstart.net

Design: Patrick Hofmann

Cover: Neda Abghari

Developed in Microsoft Word 2013

ISBN: 978-0-578-11784-3

9 8 7 6 5 4 3 2 1

Printed and bound in the United States of America

Dedication

This book is dedicated to all of my teachers and coaches. Thank you for sharing your knowledge and inspiring me to learn.

Contents

Find and replace

Footnotes and endnotes

85

91

Formatting

103

Introduction

This book was designed to help you find quick answers to common questions about Microsoft Word 2013. The sections use a question-answer format, with a short description of the question and a step-by-step solution.

The steps are written for Word 2013, but all of the information also applies to Word 2010 (except the new features, of course). If you're using Word 2013 on a touchscreen device such as a tablet, just substitute "tap" for "click"and you'll be fine.

Icons used in this book

The following icons are used throughout this book to help you find important and time-saving information.

Icon	Meaning	Description
NEW!	New	A new or drastically enhanced feature in Word 2013.
◇	Note	Additional information about a topic.
TIP▶	Tip	A recommended best practice, shortcut, or workaround.

Updates

For the most up-to-date information about this book, see www.clickstart.net or www.wordtothepoint.com.

What's new in Word 2013?

The major new features in Word 2013 are listed in the table below.

Task	See page
Using Apps	27
Opening and editing .pdf documents	219
Inserting picture from the Web	245
Inserting a video from the Web	257
Inserting a YouTube video	258
Resuming reading	276
Saving as Open Document Format (ODF 1.2)	292
Saving as Strict Open XML	293
Saving a document to the cloud	306
Sharing documents	306
Sharing on Facebook, LinkedIn, and Twitter	306
Publishing to a blog	309
Link to Flickr	310
Presenting documents on the Web	311
Defining words	329
Translating text	382
Replying to a comment	400
Expanding and collapsing headings	419

Accessibility

What is "alt" text?

Alt text specifies alternative words for a block of content that are substituted if the content is not available. Alt text is most commonly used to provide descriptions of pictures, videos, and tables. Users who have impaired vision can use a screen reader to hear the alt text for pictures, videos, and tables.

How do I add alt text to pictures?

If you add alt text to a picture, the text can be spoken by a screen reader application. Screen readers are often used by people who have a vision impairment.

To add alt text for a picture:

1   Right-click a picture and select **Format Picture**.
    The Format Picture pane appears.

2   Click the **Layout & Properties** icon.

3   Open the **ALT TEXT** section.

4   Type a **Title** for the picture and press **Enter**.

5   Type a **Description** and press **Enter**.

How do I add alt text to a table?

Like pictures, tables should include alt text for users who have a vision impairment.

To add alt text for a table:

1 Right-click inside a table and select **Table Properties**.
The Table Properties dialog box appears.

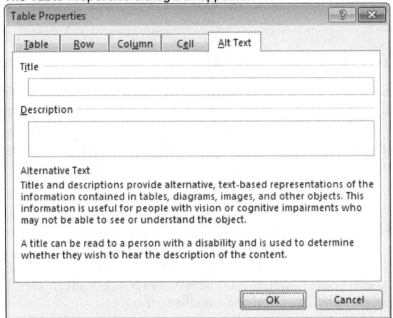

2 Select the **Alt Text** tab.

3 Type a **Title** for the table.

4 Type a **Description**.

5 Click **OK**.

How do I check a document for missing accessibility features?

Accessibility features make a document more useable for readers who have trouble seeing, hearing, or moving a mouse. For example, alt text for pictures and tables can be read aloud by a screen reader program for users who have trouble seeing. Without the alt text, these users won't have access to the picture or table.

To check for missing accessibility features:

1 Select **File** > **Info**.
   —OR—
   Press **Alt+F, I**.

2 Click the **Check for Issues** button.

3 Select **Check Accessibility**.
   A dialog box appears with a list of accessibility-related errors.

4 Click an issue in the report to move to the issue in the document.

Apps

What are apps? NEW!

Apps are additional features that can be added to Word or other Office applications. Anyone can create and share (or sell) an app that adds a new feature to Word.

To add a Web app:

1 Select the **Insert** tab.
—OR—
Press **Alt+N**.

2 Click **Apps for Office** in the **Apps** group.

3 Select **See All**.
The Insert App dialog box appears.

4 Select an app.

5 Click **Insert**.

Where can I find apps for Word? NEW!

You can download apps at:
http://goo.gl/ql7e9

Can I make my own apps? NEW!

Yes! For instructions and UI design guidelines, see
http://goo.gl/cXAX2

Autocorrect and autotext

How do I prevent automatic first-letter capitalization?

By default, Word will automatically capitalize the first letter of a sentence. This feature is normally useful, but it can be annoying if you are adding content to table cells that should not start with a capital letter.

To prevent automatic first-letter capitalization:

1   Select **File** > **Options**.
    The Word Options dialog box appears.

2   Select the **Proofing** tab.

3   In the **AutoCorrect options** section, click **AutoCorrect Options**.
    The AutoCorrect dialog box appears.

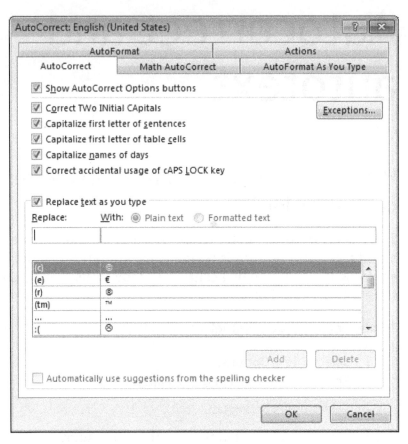

4   Select the **AutoCorrect** tab if it is not already selected.

5   Uncheck **Capitalize first letter of sentences**.

6   Click **OK**.

How do I prevent automatic dashes, fractions, and ordinals?

By default, Word will automatically convert two hyphens (--) to a dash (—), common fractions such as 1/2 to 1/2 , and ordinals such as 1st to 1st. You can turn off any of these features, if needed.

To prevent automatic dashes, fractions, and/or ordinals:

1 Select **File** > **Options.**
The Word Options dialog box appears.

2 Select the **Proofing** tab.

3 In the **AutoCorrect options** section, click **AutoCorrect Options.**
The AutoCorrect dialog box appears.

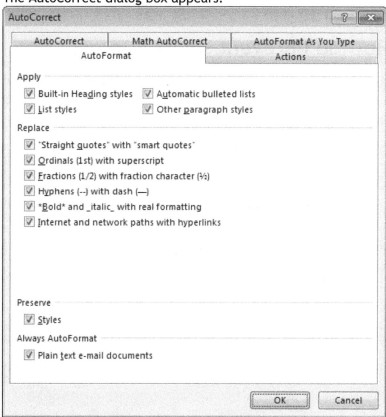

4 Select the **AutoFormat** tab.

5 In the **Replace** section, uncheck the following options:

  □ Ordinals (1st) with superscript

  □ Fractions (1/2) with fraction character

  □ Hyphens (--) with dash

6 Select the **AutoFormat As You Type** tab.

7 In the **Replace as you type** section, uncheck the following options:

    ☐ Ordinals (1st) with superscript

    ☐ Fractions (1/2) with fraction character

    ☐ Hyphens (--) with dash

8 Click **OK**.

How do I prevent smart quotes?

If you copy and paste documents containing curly or "smart quotes" into other applications, such as an HTML editor, they may appear as a rectangle (☐).

To prevent smart quotes:

1 Select **File** > **Options**.
The Word Options dialog box appears.

2 Select the **Proofing** tab.

3 In the **AutoCorrect options** section, click **AutoCorrect Options**.

The AutoCorrect dialog box appears.

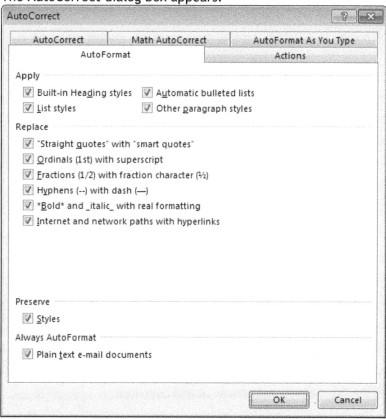

4 Select the **AutoFormat** tab.

5 In the **Replace** section, uncheck the **"Straight quotes" with "smart quotes"** option.

6 Select the **AutoFormat As You Type** tab.

7 In the **Replace as you type** section, uncheck the **"Straight quotes" with "smart quotes"** option.

8 Click **OK**.

How do I stop hyphens from becoming lines?

By default, Word will create a border if you type three hyphens and press Enter. You can turn this option off if you want to use three hyphens.

To stop hyphens from automatically being converted to a border:

1 Select **File** > **Options**.

2 Select the **Proofing** tab.

3 Click **AutoCorrect Options**.

4 Select the **AutoFormat as You Type** tab.

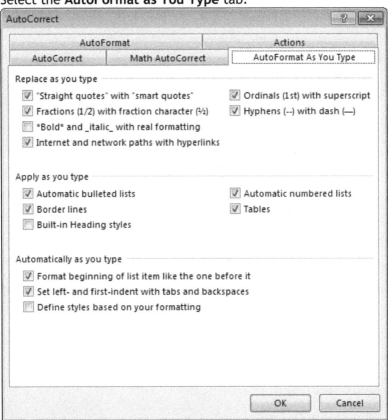

5 In the **Apply as you type** section, uncheck the **Border lines** check box.

To remove a border:

1 Click inside the paragraph.

2 Select the **Home** tab.
—OR—
Press **Alt+H**.

3 Click the ⊞ **Borders** button in the **Paragraph** group.

4 Select **No Border.**
The border will disappear.

How do I prevent smileys from changing to emoticon icons?

By default, Word will automatically convert common smileys such as :) to emoticon icons (in this case, ☺). You can turn off this feature if you would rather use smileys.

To prevent characters from being replaced with emoticons:

1 Select **File > Options.**
The Word Options dialog box appears.

2 Select the **Proofing** tab.

3 Click **AutoCorrect Options.**
The AutoCorrect dialog box appears with the AutoCorrect tab

selected.

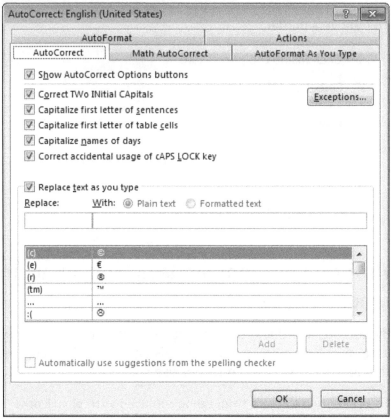

4 Select a smiley in the list.

5 Click **Delete**.
The smiley replacement option is deleted.

6 Click **OK**.

How do I create an AutoText entry?

You can create AutoText entries to insert common words or phrases. For example, an AutoText entry could insert your company's name, a website address, or a confidentiality statement. You can even include formatting in an AutoText entry.

Word displays a popup box when you start typing an AutoText entry's name. If you select the AutoText entry and press Enter, Word will insert the entry.

To create an AutoText entry:

1 Type and format your text.

2 Select the content for the AutoText entry.

3 Select the **Insert** tab.
   —OR—
   Press **Alt+N.**

4 Click the **QuickParts** button in the **Text** group.

5 Select **AutoText > Save Selection to AutoText Gallery.**
   The Create New Building Block dialog box appears.

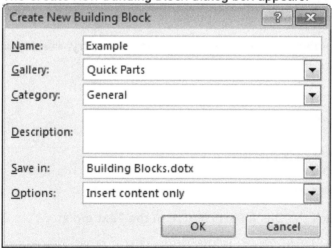

6 Type a **Name** for your AutoText entry.

7 If you plan to create numerous AutoText entries, select a **Category.**

8 For **Save in**, select a file to contain the AutoText entry.

9 For **Options**, select one of the following:

- ☐ **Insert content only** — inserts the entry inside the current paragraph

- ☐ **Insert content in its own paragraph** — inserts the entry as a new paragraph

- ☐ **Insert content in its own page** — inserts the entry as a new page

10 Click **OK**.

How do I insert an AutoText entry?

You can insert an AutoText entry by typing its name.

To insert an AutoText entry:

1 Start typing the AutoText entry's name.
A pop-up box appears.

2 Press **Enter** or **F3**.
Your autotext entry appears in your document.

TIP▶ *If you do not want to insert the AutoText entry, keep typing and the pop-will disappear.*

If you forget an AutoText entry's name:

1 Select the **Insert** tab.
—OR—
Press **Alt+N**.

2 Click the **Quick Parts** button in the **Text** group.

3 Select **AutoText**.
A list of AutoText entries appears.

4 Select an AutoText entry in the list.

How do I rename or modify an AutoText entry?

Some AutoText entries such as a copyright statement might need to be regularly updated. You can modify an AutoText entry at any time.

Updating an AutoText entry will not modify where you have previously inserted the entry.

To rename an AutoText entry:

1 Select the **Insert** tab.
—OR—
Press **Alt+N**.

2 Click the **Quick Parts** button in the **Text** group.

3 Select **Building Blocks Organizer**.
The Building Blocks Organizer dialog box appears.

4 Select an AutoText entry.

5 Click **Edit Properties**.
The Modify Building Block dialog box appears.

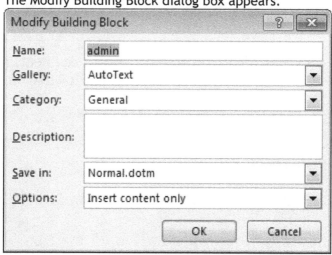

6 Type a new **Name** for the entry.

7 Click **OK** to close the Modify Building Block dialog box.

8 Click **Close** to close the Building Blocks Organizer dialog box.

How do I delete an AutoText entry?

If you no longer need an AutoText entry, you can delete it.

To delete an AutoText entry:

1　Select the **Insert** tab.
　—OR—
　Press **Alt+N**.

2　Click the **Quick Parts** button in the **Text** group.

3　Select **Building Blocks Organizer**.
　The Building Blocks Organizer dialog box appears.

4　Select an AutoText entry.

5　Click **Delete**.

6　Click **Yes**.
　The Autotext entry is deleted.

7　Click **Close**.

How can I insert text with a shortcut key?

You can use the AutoCorrect feature to replace a short string of characters, such as "cs," with your copyright statement. It's not quite as simple as pressing a shortcut key, but it works well.

To insert text by typing a short string of characters:

1　Select **File** > **Options**.
　The Word Options dialog box appears.

2 Select the **Proofing** tab.

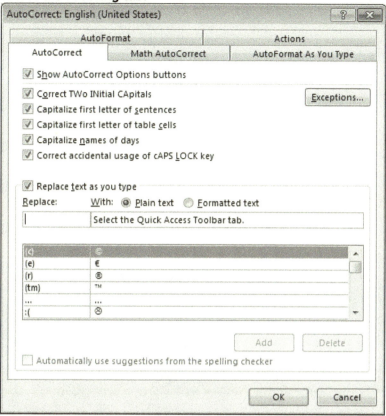

3 Select the **AutoCorrect** tab.

4 For **Replace**, type the text string you want to replace.

5 For **With**, type the text that should replace the text string.

6 Click **Add**.

7 Click **OK**.

Copy and paste

How do I copy and paste using the keyboard?

When you copy content, the new content usually replaces the content that is in your clipboard. If you use the keyboard, you can copy content without replacing what is in your clipboard.

To copy and paste using the keyboard:

1 Highlight the content you want to copy.

2 Press **Shift+F2**.
  The **Copy to where?** Message appears in the lower left corner of the status bar.

3 Move the insertion point to where you want to paste the content.

4 Press **Enter**.

If you want to move text instead, press **F2** instead of **Shift+F2**.

What is the spike?

The spike is an alternative to the clipboard. The clipboard can only contain one selection, but the spike can contain numerous entries that you can paste into a document. When the content of the spike is pasted into a document, it's pasted in the order that it was spiked.

To add content to the spike:

1 Select the content.

2 Press **Ctrl+F3**.

3   To paste the content from the spike, press **Ctrl+Shift+F3**.

To paste the content of the spike into a document and retain it in the spike, type **spike** and press **F3**.

How do I control the formatting when I paste?

When you copy and paste content, you can specify whether the pasted content should include or not include its formatting. If you paste between documents, you can specify whether the formatting matches the source document or the new document.

To set the default formatting when pasting text:

1   Select **File > Options**.

2   Select the **Advanced** tab.

3   Scroll down to the **Cut, copy, and paste** section.

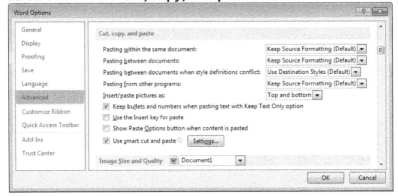

4   Set the **Pasting within the same document** option.

5   Set the **Pasting between documents** option.

6   Set the **Pasting between documents when style definitions conflict** option.

7   Click **Settings** beside **Use smart copy and paste**.

The Settings dialog box appears.

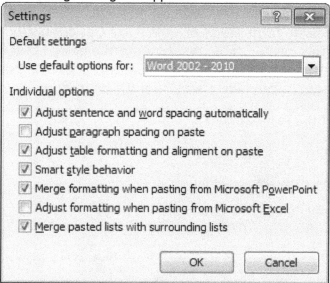

8 Select the **Individual options** as desired.

9 Click **OK**.

How do I copy formatting and not text?

You can copy formatting from a paragraph (or content in a paragraph) and apply it to other content in a document. For example, you could copy the formatting for a "Tip" and apply it to another tip.

To copy formatting and not text:

1 Highlight the content.

2 Press **Ctrl+Shift+C** instead of **Ctrl+C**.
The formatting is copied.

3 Select the content to which the formatting is to be applied.

4 Press **Ctrl+Shift+V** to apply the formatting to the selection.

How do I turn off the paste options?

When you paste formatted text, the Paste Options button appears. This menu can be used to make the pasted text match the formatting of the destination document, but some users find it annoying. You can hide the menu if it's distracting.

To turn off the Paste Options menu:

1 Select **File** > **Options**.

2 Select the **Advanced** tab.

3 Scroll down to the **Cut, copy, and paste** section.

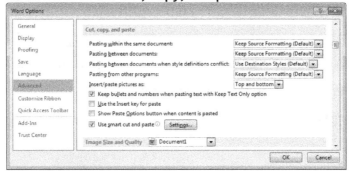

4 Uncheck the **Show Paste Options button when content is pasted** check box.

5 Click **OK**.

Envelopes and mailings

How do I create envelopes?

You can create and print envelopes, including the address, return address, and a stamp placeholder.

To create an envelope:

1   Select the **Mailings** tab.
   —OR—
   Press **Alt+M**.

2   Click the **Envelopes** button in the **Create** group.

   The Envelopes and Labels dialog box appears.

3 Select the **Envelopes** tab.

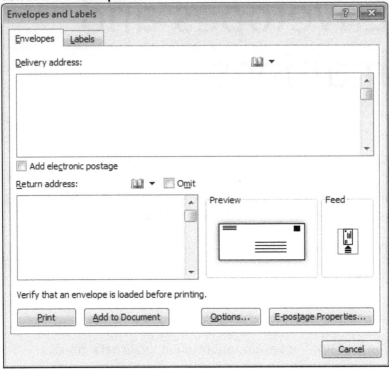

4 Type a **Delivery address**.
If Word finds an address near the top of your document, it adds the address to the Delivery address box. You can change it, if needed.

5 Type a **Return address**.

6 Click **Print**.
A dialog box appears if you typed a return address.

7 If you typed a return address, click **Yes** to save the address.
If you save the return address, Word can include it each time you print an envelope.

How do I add an address for envelopes?

Word uses the "Envelope Address" and "Envelope Return" styles to format the envelope. You can modify these styles if needed.

To add an address for an envelope:

1   Select the **Home** tab.
    —OR—
    Press **Alt+H**.

2   Click the ⌐ small arrow in the lower-right corner of the **Styles** group.
    —OR—
    Press **Shift+Ctrl+Alt+S**.
    The Styles pane appears.

3   Click **Options** at the bottom of the Styles pane.
    The Style Pane Options dialog box appears.

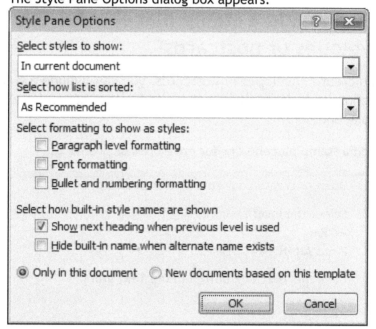

4   For **Select Styles to Show**, select **All Styles**.

5   Click **OK** to close the Style Pane Options dialog box.

6   Click the arrow to the right of the **Envelop Address** style's name and select **Modify**.
    The Modify Style dialog box appears.

7   Click **Format** and select **Font**.
    The Font dialog box appears.

8 Change the font information, as desired.

9 Click **OK** to close the Font dialog box appears.

10 Select the **New Documents Based On this Template** option.

11 Click **OK**.

12 Repeat steps 6-11 to modify the Envelope Return style, if desired.

When you save your document or close Word, you can save your changes to these envelope styles to your template.

How do I add a stamp placeholder for envelopes or postcards?

If you create envelopes or postcards, you can include a stamp placeholder. In fact, you can even add "place stamp here" to the placeholder.

To add a stamp placeholder for envelopes or postcards:

1 Open or create your envelope or postcard.

2 Select the **Insert** tab.
—OR—
Press **Alt+N**.

3 Click the **Text Box** button in the **Text** group.

4 Select **Draw Text Box**.
The mouse pointer changes to a crosshair.

5 Click where you want to place the upper-left corner of the placeholder.

6 Drag the mouse to the lower-right corner of the placeholder. When you release the mouse, the text box is inserted.

7 Right-click the text box and select **More Layout Options**. The Layout dialog box appears.

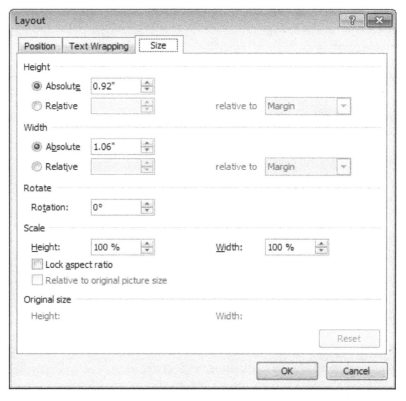

8 Select the **Size** tab.

9 Set the **Height** value to 1 inch.

10 Set the **Width** value to .75 inch.

11 Click **OK**.

12 Click inside the text box.

13 Type the text you want to appear within the placeholder. For example: Place stamp here

14 Format the text as desired.

TIP▶ *You will probably need to make the font size smaller so the text is completely visible.*

How do I set the margin for envelopes?

You can set the top and left margins for the address and the return address to specify where the addresses print on your envelopes.

To set margins for envelopes:

1 Select the **Mailings** tab.
   —OR—
   Press **Alt+M**.

2 Click the **Envelopes** button in the **Create** group.

   The Envelopes and Labels dialog box appears with the Envelopes tab selected.

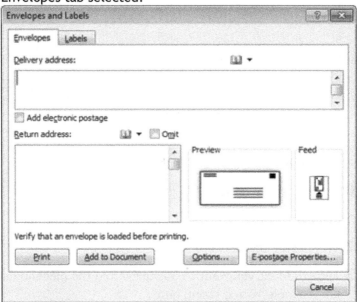

3 Click **Options**.
   The Envelope Options dialog box appears.

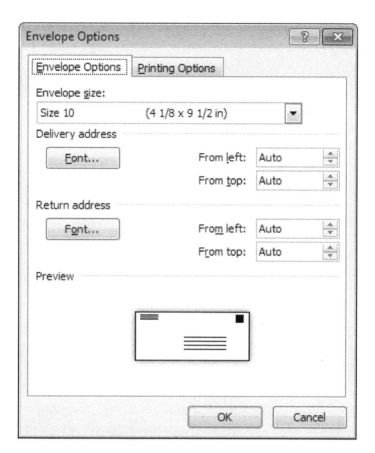

4 Select the **Envelope Options** tab.

5 Change the positioning of the addresses, as desired.

6 Click **OK** to close the Envelope Options dialog box appears.

7 Click **Add to Document**.
   The envelope appears in your document.

TIP *If you set the margins in a template, any documents that use the template will use your envelope settings.*

Fields

How do I use fields?

You can use fields to add a bar codes, symbols, document information such as the author's name, and other content.

1 Select the **Insert** tab.
—OR—
Press **Alt+N**.

2 Click the **Quick Parts** button in the **Text** group.

3 Select **Field**.
The Field dialog box appears.

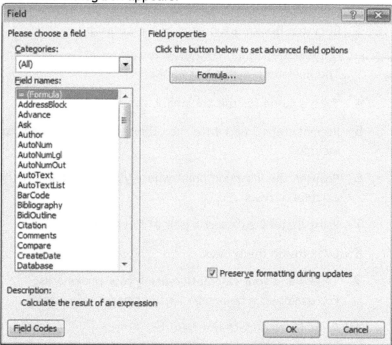

4 Select the field you want to insert.

5 Click **OK**.
The field is inserted into your document.

How do I calculate field totals?

You can calculate totals or other results for numbers that appear anywhere in a document. For example, you could calculate a yearly total based on monthly sales numbers.

To calculate results based on numbers in a document:

1 Highlight the first number that you want to include in the calculation.
 If your number is a currency value, do not highlight the currency symbol (such as $).

2 Select the **Insert** tab.
—OR—
Press **Alt+N**.

3 Click the **Bookmark** button in the **Links** group.
⚑ Bookmark
The Bookmark dialog box appears.

4 Type a name for the bookmark and click **OK**.

5 Repeat steps 3 and 4 for the other numbers you want to include.

6 Position the insertion point where you want to insert the calculated result.

7 Press **Ctrl+F9** to insert a pair of field braces.

8 Click inside the braces.

9 Type = and your calculation using your bookmarks.
For example: = bookmark1 + bookmark2

10 Press **F9** to update the field.
The calculation appears in your document. If you change the amounts, the calculated result will be updated when you press F9.

How do I update fields?

If you use fields (including a table of contents and index), you can update all of the field results at the same time.

To update the fields in a document:

1 Press **Ctrl+A**.
All of the content in your document is highlighted.

2 Press **F9**.

How do I insert the date the document was last saved?

You can use the **SaveDate** field to include the date the document was last saved.

To insert the date the document was last saved:

1 Position the insertion point where you want the date to appear.

2 Select the **Insert** tab.
—OR—
Press **Alt+N**.

3 Click the **Quick Parts** button in the **Text** group.

4 Select **Field**.

The Field dialog box appears.

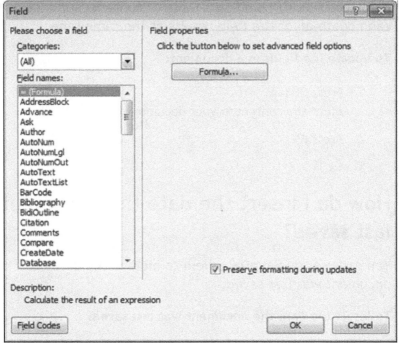

5 In the **Categories** list, select **Date and Time**.

6 Select **SaveDate** in the **Field names** list.

7 Select a **Date Format**.

8 Click **OK**.

How do I insert the date the document was last printed?

You can use the **PrintDate** field to include the date the document was last printed. For example, you could include a "last printed" heading on a cover page to track the last printed version of the document.

To insert the last date the document was printed:

1   Position the insertion point where you want to insert the date.

2   Select the **Insert** tab.
    —OR—
    Press **Alt+N**.

3   Click the **Quick Parts** button in the **Text** group.

4   Select **Field**.
    The Field dialog box appears.

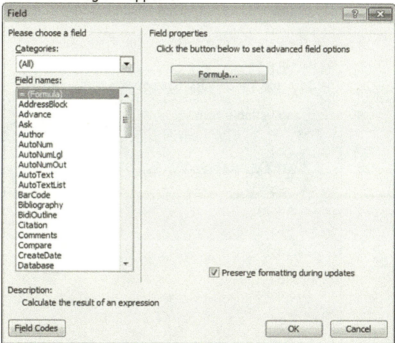

5   In the **Categories** list, select **Document Information**.

6   Select **PrintDate** in the **Field names** list.

7   Select a **Date Format**.

8   Click **OK**.

How do I create a shortcut to insert the date?

You can create a Building Block to insert the date using your preferred date format.

To create a Building Block to insert the date:

1   Position the insertion point on a blank line.

2   Select the **Insert** tab.
  —OR—
  Press **Alt+N**.

3   Click the **Date & Time** button in the **Text** group.

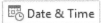 Date & Time

  The Date and Time dialog box appears.

4   Select an **Available format**.

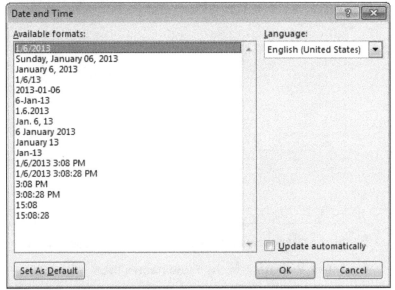

5   Select the **Update automatically** check box.

6   Click **OK**.
  The date appears in your document.

7   Select the date field and press **Shift+F9**.
  The field code appears.

8 Select the date field.

9 Press **Alt+F3**.
The Create New Building Block dialog box appears.

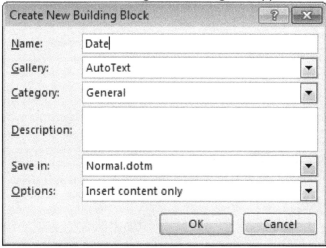

10 In the **Name** field, type **Date**.

11 Click **OK**.
Your Date field, properly formatted, is now saved in a Building Block entry named "Date."

To use the entry, type the word Date and press **Enter**. The word Date will be replaced with your Date field.

How do I stop an inserted date or time from auto-updating?

If you insert a date or time, you can specify whether it automatically updates to the current date or time or maintains the date or time from when it was inserted.

To stop an inserted date or time from auto-updating:

1 Select the **Insert** tab.
—OR—
Press **Alt+N**.

2   Click the **Date & Time** button in the **Text** group.

The Date and Time dialog box appears.

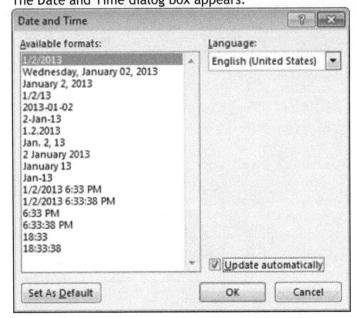

3   Select an **Available format**.

4   Uncheck the **Update automatically** check box.

5   Click **OK**.

How do I insert a document's location?

You can use the **FileName** field to include a document's location. For example, you could include the document's location and filename in the footer so your readers know where the document is stored.

To insert a document's location:

1   Position the insertion point where you to insert the path.

2   Select the **Insert** tab.

   —OR—

   Press **Alt+N**.

3 Click the **Quick Parts** button in the **Text** group.

|□| Quick Parts ▾

4 Select **Field**.
The Field dialog box appears.

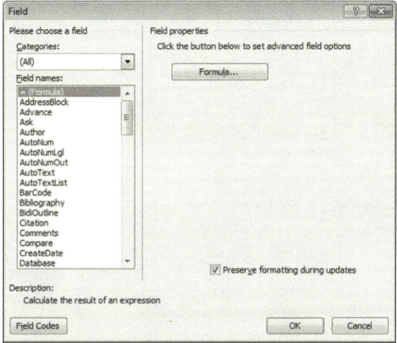

5 In the **Categories** list, select **Document Information**.

6 For **Field names**, select **FileName**.

7 Click **Field Codes**.

8 Click **Options**.
The Field Options dialog box appears.

9 Select the **Field Specific Switches** tab.

10 For **Switches,** select **\p.**

11 Click **Add to Field.**

12 Click **OK** to close the Field Options dialog box appears.

13 Click **OK** to close the Field dialog box and insert the field.

How do I insert a document's filename?

You can use the FileName field to insert a document's path and filename.

To insert a document's filename:

1 Press **Ctrl+F9.**
   The field code braces appear.

2 Inside the braces, type:
   FILENAME \p * MERGEFORMAT

The \p switch includes the file path. You can leave it out if you only want to insert the filename.

3   Position the insert point inside the braces and press **F9**.

4   To hide the filename, highlight it and press **Shift+Ctrl+H**.

How do I insert a document's size?

You can use the **FileSize** field to insert a document's size. For example, you might include the file size as part of a document summary page.

A document's file size is larger than the number of characters in the document. The document also includes "internal" information that does not display, such as how the document is formatted and the name of the theme and/or template it uses.

To insert a document's size in a document:

1   Position the insertion point where you want to insert the file size.

2   Select the **Insert** tab.
    —OR—
    Press **Alt+N**.

3   Click the **Quick Parts** button in the **Text** group.

4 Select **Fields**.

The Field dialog box appears.

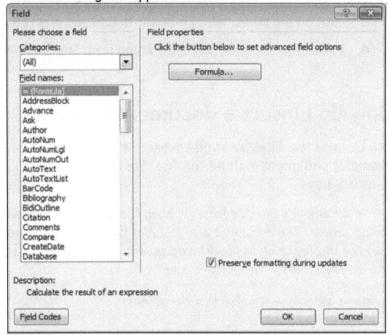

5 In the **Categories** list, select **Document Information**.

6 Select **FileSize** in the **Field Names** list.

7 Click **OK**.

How do I insert the document's author or title?

You can use the **DocProperty** field to include the author, subject, title, keywords, last modified date, number of characters, number of pages, and other information.

To insert document properties:

1 Position the insertion point where you want the summary information to be inserted.

2   Select the **Insert** tab.
  —OR—
  Press **Alt+N.**

3   Click the **Quick Parts** button in the **Text** group.

4   Select **Field.**
  The Field dialog box appears.

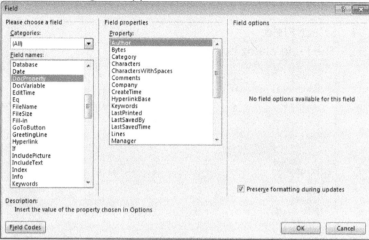

5   In the **Categories** list, select **DocProperty.**

6   Select a **Property.**

7   Click **OK.**

How do I insert custom document properties?

Word automatically tracks document properties such as the file size, number of words, and last modified date. You can add other properties, such as the document's title, by selecting **File > Info.**

Word includes built-in fields to insert the default properties, but you can also insert a custom property's value.

To insert a custom property's value:

1   Position the insertion point where you want to insert the field.

2   Select the **Insert** tab.
    —OR—
    Press **Alt+N**.

3   Click the **Quick Parts** button in the **Text** group.

4   Select **Field**.
    The Field dialog box appears.

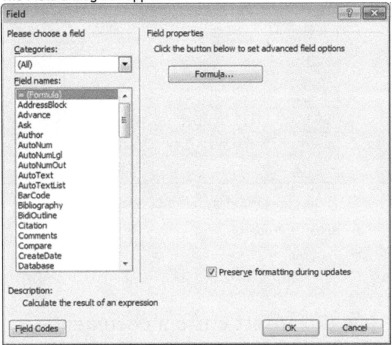

5   In the list of **Categories**, select **Document Information**.

6   For **Field Names**, select **DocProperty**.

7   In the **Property** list, select your custom property.

8   Click **OK**.
    Word inserts the custom property's value into your document.

How do I insert the total number of pages in a document?

You can use the **NumPages** field to insert the total number of pages in a document. For example, you might create a footer that includes the current page number and total page count.

To insert the total number of pages in a document:

1 Position the insertion point where you want the total number of pages to appear.

2 Select the **Insert** tab.
—OR—
Press **Alt+N**.

3 Click the **Quick Parts** button in the **Text** group.

4 Select **Field**.
The Field dialog box appears.

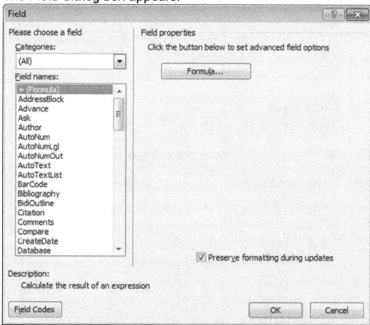

5 In the **Categories** drop-down list, select **Document Information**.

6   In the **Field Names** list, select **NumPages**.

7   Click **OK**.
The field is inserted.

How do I insert a document revision number?

Word has a built-in "revision number" that increases each time you save a document. The revision number is probably not that useful—I rarely use it. However, you can insert it into a document if needed.

To insert the document revision number:

1   Position the insertion point where you want the revision number to appear.

2   Select the **Insert** tab.
—OR—
Press **Alt+N**.

3   Click the **Quick Parts** button in the **Text** group.

4   Select **Field**.
The Field dialog box appears.

5   Select **Numbering** from the **Categories** list.

6   In the **Field Names** list, select **RevNum**.

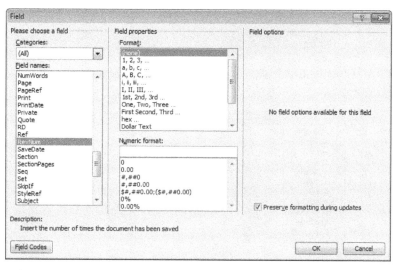

7 Select a **Format**.

8 Click **OK**.
The field is inserted into your document.

How do I insert my address?

You can use the **UserAddress** field to insert your address into a document.

To insert your address:

1 Position the insertion point where you want to insert the address.

2 Select the **Insert** tab.
—OR—
Press **Alt+N**.

3 Click the **Quick Parts** button in the **Text** group.

4 Select **Field.**
The Field dialog box appears.

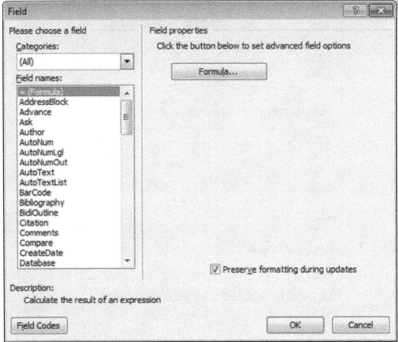

5 In the **Categories** drop-down list, select **User Information.**

6 In the **Field Names** list, select **UserAddress.**

7 Click **OK**
The field is inserted.

How do I insert my initials?

You can use the **UserInitials** field to insert your initials into a document.

To specify your initials:

1 Select **File** > **Options.**
The Word Options dialog box appears.

2 Select the **General** tab.

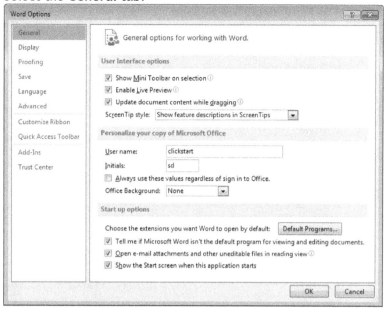

3 Modify the information in the **Initials** box.

4 Click **OK**.

To insert your initials into a document:

1 Position the insertion point where you want to insert your initials.

2 Select the **Insert** tab.
—OR—
Press **Alt+N**.

3 Click the **Quick Parts** button in the **Text** group.

4 Select **Field**.

The Field dialog box appears.

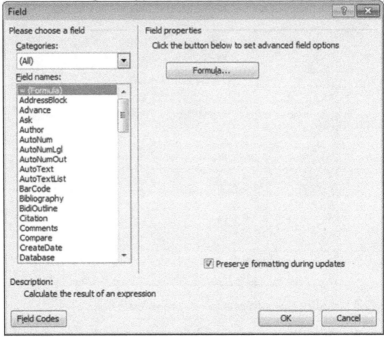

5 In the **Categories** drop-down list, select **User Information**.

6 In the **Field Names** list, select **UserInitials**.

7 Click **OK**.

The field is inserted.

How do I insert my name?

You can use the **UserName** field to insert your name into a document. For example, you might insert your name when you are writing a letter or creating an envelope. If you update your name (select the **File** tab and click the **Author** field), your name will be updated throughout your document.

To insert the author's name:

1 Position the insertion point where you want to insert the user's name.

2 Select the **Insert** tab.
—OR—
Press **Alt+N**.

3 Click the **Quick Parts** button in the **Text** group.

4 Select **Field**.
The Field dialog box appears.

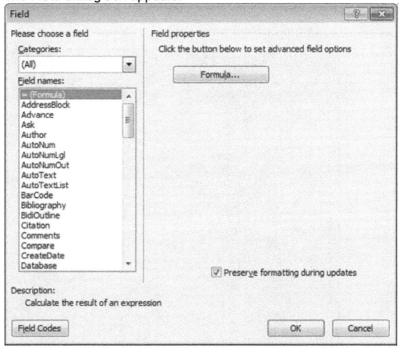

5 In the **Categories** list, select **User Information**.

6 In the **Field Names** list, select **UserName**.

7 Click **OK**.

How do I insert a phone number?

You can add a custom **Telephone Number** field to insert a phone number into a document.

To add a phone number:

1 Select **File** > **Info**.

2 Click **Properties** on the right side of the window.

   Properties ▾

3 Select **Advanced Properties**.
   The Properties dialog box appears.

4 Select the **Custom** tab.

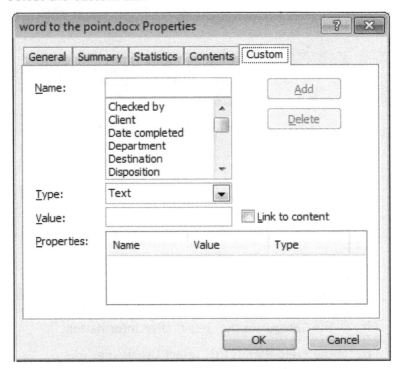

5 In the list of properties, select **Telephone Number**.

6 For **Value**, type a phone number.

7 Click **Add**.

8 Click **OK**.

To insert the phone number:

1 Position the insertion point where you want to insert the phone number.

2 Select the **Insert** tab.
—OR—
Press **Alt+N**.

3 Click the **Quick Parts** button in the **Text** group.

4 Select **Field**.
The Field dialog box appears.

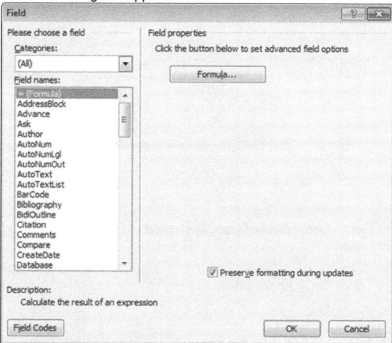

5 In the **Categories** drop-down list, select **All**.

6 In the **Field Names** list, select **DocProperty**.

7 In the **Field Properties** list, select **Telephone number**.

8 Click **OK**.
The field is inserted.

How do I print field codes?

If you insert fields into a document, you can print a version of the document with the field codes visible. Printing the field codes could be useful to show another user which fields you are using or to troubleshoot an issue with a field.

To print a document with field codes:

1 Select **File** > **Options**.
   The Word Options dialog box appears.

2 Select the **Advanced** tab.

3 Scroll down to the **Print** section.

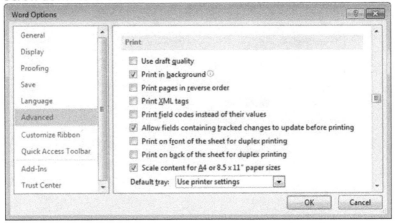

4 Select **Print field codes instead of their values**.

5 Click **OK**.

6 Print your document.

How do I include content from another document?

You can use the **IncludeText** field and a bookmark to include text from another document.

To include content from another document:

1 Open the source document.

2 Add a bookmark for the content you want to include (**Insert** >
  Bookmark).

3 Position the cursor in your document where you want to insert
  the content.

4 Press **Ctrl+F9**.
  The field braces appear.

5 Inside the braces, type:
  INCLUDETEXT "c:\\SampleFolder\\MyFile.doc" *BookmarkName*

  where "BookmarkName" is the name of the bookmark

6 Press **Shift+F9**.
  The field code is replaced by the inserted content.

How do I find a field?

If you insert a field into a document and view the field results, it
can be hard to find the field since it looks like regular content.
You can use the Find and Replace dialog box to find a field if you
need to modify, update, or delete it.

To find a field:

1 If you are viewing the field results in your document, press
  Alt+F9 to display the field codes.

2 Press **Ctrl+H**.
  The Find and Replace dialog box appears.

3 For **Find what**, type ^d *yourfieldsname*
  where *yourfieldsname* is the field you want to find

4 Click **Find Next**.

How do I select a field?

You may need to select a field to move it to another location, modify it, or to delete it.

To select a field:

- ☐ If the field results are visible, select the first character of the field.

- ☐ If the field codes are visible, select the opening brace: {

To switch between viewing field codes and their results, press **Alt+F9**.

How do I highlight fields?

By default, Word will highlight a field (or its result) when you move the insert point inside the field. You can turn off the highlighting if you find it distracting. If you like the highlighting, you can set Word to always highlight fields.

To highlight fields:

1 Select **File** > **Options**.
  The Word Options dialog box appears.

2 Select the **Advanced** tab.

3 Scroll down to the **Show document content** section.

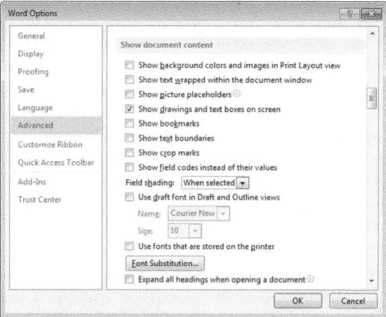

4 In the **Field shading** drop-down list, specify how you want Word to handle field shading.

5 Click **OK**.

How do I delete all of the fields in a document?

You can replace all of the fields in a document with their results, or you can completely delete the field and their results.

To replace all of the fields with their text results:

1 Press **Ctrl+A** to select the entire document.

2 Press **Ctrl+Shift+F**.
The fields are replaced with the results of the field calculation.

To delete all fields:

1 Press **Alt+F9**. This makes all the field codes in your document visible, instead of the results of those fields.

2 Press **Ctrl+H**.
   The Find and Replace dialog box appears with the Replace tab selected.

3 For **Find what**, type **^d** (make sure you use a lowercase d). ^d is the code for fields.

4 Leave the **Replace with** box empty.

5 Click **Replace All**.

Where can I learn more about fields?

Word's online help provides descriptions about fields and examples of using them in a document.

To view help for fields:

1 Select the **Insert** tab.
   —OR—
   Press **Alt+N**.

2 Click the **Quick Parts** button in the **Text** group.

3 Select **Field**.

The Field dialog box appears.

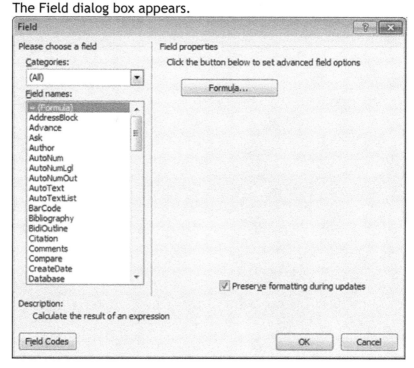

4 Select one of the field **Categories**.

5 Select a **Field name**.

6 Click the ⟨?⟩ question mark icon in the upper-right corner of the Field dialog box.

The Word Help window appears.

Find and replace

How do I find within a selection?

Normally, the Find and Find and Replace features will search the entire document. To find only within a section of a document, highlight the content you want to search, then press **Ctrl+F** (find) or **Ctrl+H** (find and replace).

How do I count uses of a word?

You can use the Find feature to count how many times a word or phrase is used.

To create a word count:

1 Press **Ctrl+F**.
   The Navigation pane appears.

2 Type the word or phrase you want to count and press **Enter**.
   Word display a list of where the word or phrase is used in the document and a count of how often it appears.

How do I find special characters?

You can also use the Find feature to find special characters such as paragraph marks, non-breaking spaces, and hyphens.

To find special characters:

1 Press **Ctrl+H**.
   The Find and Replace dialog box appears.

2 Click the **Find** tab.

3 Position the cursor in the **Find what** box.

4   If the dialog box is not expanded, click **More**.

5   Click **Special**.

6   Select a special character.

7   Click **Find Next**.

How do I find breaks?

You can the Find and Replace feature to find and replace section, page, column, and line breaks.

To find breaks:

1   Press **Ctrl+F**.
    The Navigation task pane appears.

2   In the box at the top of the Navigation pane, type **^l** to find line breaks, **^m** to find page breaks, **^n** to find column breaks, or **^s** to find section breaks.

How do I find formatting?

You can find and replace formatting, such as boldfacing, italicizing, colors, or styles.

To find formatting:

1   Press **Ctrl+H**.
    The Find and Replace dialog box appears.

2   Position the cursor in the **Find what** box.

3   If the dialog box is not expanded, click **More**.

4   Click **Format**.

5   Do one of the following:

    ☐   To find character-level formatting, such as boldfacing, select **Font**.

- To find paragraph-level formatting such as indents, select **Paragraph**.

- To find a style, select **Style**.

6 Select the formatting or style you want to find and click **OK**.

7 Click **Find Next**.

How do I find the next match?

You can press **Shift+F4** to find the next match, even if the Navigation pane or Find and Replace dialog box is closed.

How do I find and add additional text?

You can use a regular expression to find text and add additional text. For example, you could find "Microsoft Word" and replace it with "Microsoft Word 2013."

To find and add additional text:

1 Press **Ctrl+H**.
The Find and Replace dialog box appears.

2 For **Find what**, type the text you want to find.

3 For **Replace with**, type ^& and the text you want to add. For example, ^& **2013**.

4 Click **Find Next** or **Replace All**.

How do I replace multiple spaces with a tab?

You can also use a regular expression to find and replace multiple spaces with a tab.

To replace multiple spaces with a tab:

1   Press **Ctrl+H**.
    The Find and Replace dialog box appears.

2   For **Find what**, type a space followed by **{2,}**.
    {2,} is a regular expression for two or more spaces.

3   For **Replace with**, type **^t**
    ^t represents a tab.

4   Click **Find Next** or **Replace All**.

How do I replace text with a picture?

You can replace text with a picture, such as a company name with a logo.

To replace text with a picture:

1   Select the graphic.

2   Press **Ctrl+C**.

3   Press **Ctrl+H**.
    The Find and Replace dialog box appears with the Replace tab selected.

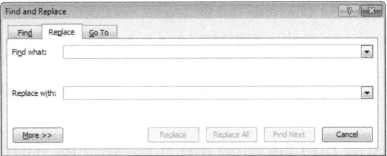

4   For **Find what**, type the text you want to replace.

5   For **Replace with**, type **^c**
    ^c represents the clipboard's contents.

6   Click **Find Next** or **Replace All**.

How do I replace a picture with another picture?

You can use the Find and Replace feature to find and replace pictures with a new picture.

To replace a picture with a picture:

1 Select the new picture and press **Ctrl+C**.

2 Press **Ctrl+H**.
The Find and Replace dialog box appears.

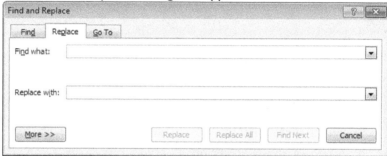

3 For **Find what**, type **^g**.
^g represents any graphics in a document.

4 For **Replace with**, type **^c**.
^c represents the clipboard's contents.

5 If you only want to replace some of the pictures, click **Find Next**. If you want to replace all of the pictures, click **Replace All**.

How do I find and copy all of the matches?

You can use the Find feature to find and select all of find results in a document. For example, you could find all of the italicized text or all of the content that uses a specific style.

To find and copy all of the matches:

1 Press **Ctrl+H**.
The Find and Replace dialog box appears with the Replace tab selected.

2 Select the **Find** tab.

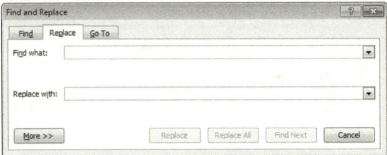

3 For **Find what**, type the text you would like to find.

4 Click **Reading Highlight**.

5 Select **Highlight All**.
All of the matches are highlighted.

6 Click **Close**.

Footnotes and endnotes

How do I create a footnote?

You can create a footnote to include a reference or citation in a technical or research-based document.

To create a footnote:

1   Position your cursor where you want to add the footnote.

2   Select the **References** tab.
    —OR—
    Press **Alt+S**.

3   Click the **Insert Footnote** button in the **Footnotes** group.

4   The footnote number appears in your document and the footnote appears at the bottom of the page.

5   Type the footnote.

How do I create an endnote?

You can create an endnote for references and citations. Endnotes are often used for longer citations since they appear at the end of a document instead of at the bottom of the page like footnotes.

To create an endnote:

1   Position your cursor where you want to add the endnote reference.

2   Select the **References** tab.
    —OR—
    Press **Alt+S.**

3   Click the **Insert Endnote** button in the **Footnotes** group.

 Insert Endnote

4   The endnote number appears in your document and the endnote appears at the end of the document.

5   Type the endnote.

How do I convert footnotes to endnotes?

You can convert between footnotes and endnotes in a document, which could be required if you switch between style guides.

To convert between footnotes and endnotes:

1   Select the **References** tab.
    —OR—
    Press **Alt+S.**

2   Click the ⌐ small arrow in the lower-right corner of the **Footnotes** group.

The Footnote and Endnote dialog box appears.

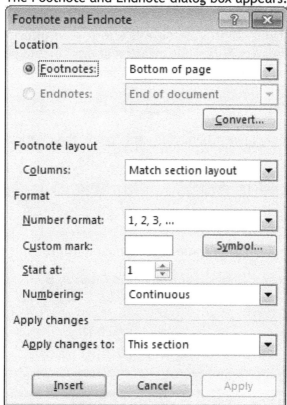

3 Click **Convert**.

The Convert Notes dialog box appears.

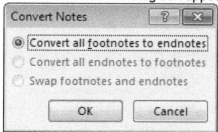

4 Select a conversion option.

5 Click **OK**.

How do I create a citation?

You can add citations to provide details about your information sources. Word supports numerous citation styles, including APA, Chicago Manual of Style, IEEE, and MLA.

To create a citation:

1 Position your cursor where you want to add the citation reference.

2 Select the **References** tab.
   —OR—
   Press **Alt+S**.

3 Select a **Style** in the **Citations & Bibliography** group.

4 Click the **Insert Citation** button in the **Citation & Bibliography** group.

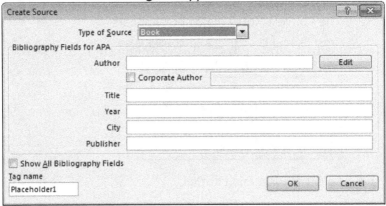

5 Select **Add New Source**.
   The Create Source dialog box appears.

6 Select a **Type of Source**.

7 Type the **Bibliographic Fields**.
   The fields will vary based on your selected citation style and the type of reference.

8 Click **OK**.
The citation appears in your document.

How do I update citation formats?

In previous versions of Word, you had to wait for a new version if there was a change to a citation format or a new format was created. When you open Word 2013, it automatically checks to see if a new citation format is available or if a format has been updated. Any new formats or changes are automatically downloaded to your PC and can be applied to your documents.

How do I create a bibliography?

If your document contains citations, you can combine them into a bibliography.

To create a bibliography:

1 Position your cursor where you want to add the bibliography.

2 Select the **References** tab.
—OR—
Press **Alt+S**.

3 Click the **Bibliography** button in the **Citation & Bibliography** group.

4 Click a Bibliography design.
The bibliography appears in your document.

How do I add brackets around footnotes?

Many style guides require brackets around footnote references. You can use the Find and Replace feature to add brackets around footnotes.

To add brackets around footnotes:

1 Press **Ctrl+H**.
The Find and Replace dialog box appears with the Replace tab selected.

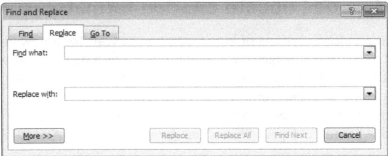

2 For **Find what**, type ^f.
^f is the code for footnotes.

3 For **Replace with**, type **[^&]**.

4 Click **Replace All**.
Brackets are added around your footnotes.

How do I change footnote numbering?

Footnotes numbers automatically start with "1," but you can change the starting number.

To change the footnote numbering:

1 Select the **References** tab.
—OR—
Press **Alt+S**.

2 Click the ⌐ small arrow in the lower-right corner of the **Footnotes** group.

The Footnote and Endnote dialog box appears.

3   For **Location**, select **Footnotes**.

4   Set the **Number format**.

5   Select a **Start at** value.

6   Click **Apply** to save the settings.

7   Click **Cancel**.

How do I specify where footnotes are placed?

By default, footnotes appear at the bottom of the page. On the last page of a document, you may decide to have your footnotes appear below the text rather than at the very bottom of the page.

To specify where Word places footnotes:

1 Select the **Reference** tab.

2 Click the ⌐ small arrow in the lower-right corner of the **Footnotes** group.
The Footnote and Endnote dialog box appears.

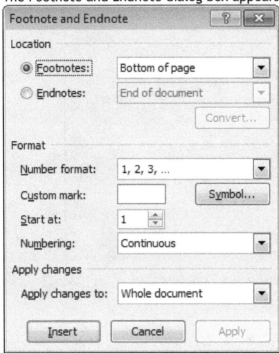

3 For **Location**, select **Footnotes**.

4 In the drop-down list to the right of the **Location**, select where you want to place your footnotes.

5 Click **Apply** to save your changes.

6 Click **Cancel**.

How do I create multiple references to the same footnote?

You can use bookmarks to create multiple references to the same footnote and endnote. This approach allows you to avoid repeating a footnote or endnote, and it is required by many scientific journals and style guides.

To create multiple references to a footnote:

1 Insert the first footnote.

2 Position the insertion point in the document where you want to add the second reference to the footnote.

3 Select the **References** tab.
—OR—
Press **Alt+S**.

4 Click the **Cross-reference** button in the **Captions** group.

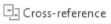

The Cross-reference dialog box appears.

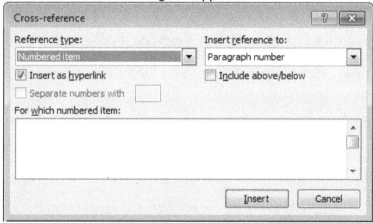

5 For **Reference Type**, select **Footnote** or **Endnote**.
A list of footnotes appears.

6 Select the first footnote or endnote you added.

7 Click **Insert**.
The cross-reference is inserted, but it is not formatted as a footnote or endnote.

8 Click **Close**.

9 Select the cross-reference.

10 Press **Shift+F9**.

The contents of the cross reference field appears. For example: { REF _Ref12345 \h }

11 Position the insertion point between the last space and the closing brace in the field.

12 Type \f.

\f is the switch to use the same formatting as your other footnote references. For example: { REF _Ref12345 \h \f }

13 Press **Shift+F9** to hide the field.

14 Press **F9** to update the field's content.

To update cross-reference fields, press **Ctrl+A** to select the entire document and press **F9**.

How do I move to a footnote?

You can quickly move to a specific footnote using the Go To feature.

To move to a footnote:

1 Press **F5**.

The Find and Replace dialog box appears with the Go To tab selected.

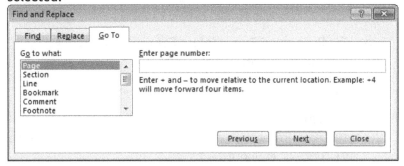

2 For **Go to what**, select **Footnote**.

3 In the **Enter Footnote Number** box, type the footnote number to which you want to move.

If you want to go to the next footnote, leave the box blank.

4 Click **Go To.**

—OR—

If you left the Enter Footnote Number blank, click **Next.**

—OR—

If you want to move to a footnote relative to the one you are currently viewing, type + or - and a number. For example, type +2 to move forward two footnotes.

> ◇ *If there are no footnotes in the document, or if you enter an invalid footnote number, Word will move to the beginning of the document.*

5 Click **Close.**

How do I delete footnotes?

You can use the Find and Replace feature to delete all of the footnotes in a document.

To delete footnotes:

1 Press **Ctrl+H.**

The Find and Replace dialog box appears with the Replace tab selected.

2 For **Find what**, type ^f

^f is the code for footnotes.

3 For **Replace with**, leave the textbox empty.

4 Click **Replace All.**

Formatting

Why should I use heading styles?

You can create your own styles to use for headings (for example, "ChapterTitle" or "SectionTitle"), but the following Word features assume you are using the built-in Heading 1-9 styles:

Feature	How the built-in Heading styles help
Chapter numbering for headings, pages, or captions	If you plan to use "chapter" numbering, Word can automatically continue or restart numbering based on the Heading 1-9 styles.
Hyperlinks and cross references	The "Place in This Document" option in the Hyperlinks dialog box and the "Headings" option in the Cross References dialog box automatically use the Heading 1-9 styles.
Keyboard shortcuts	The Heading 1-9 styles are automatically assigned to the Alt+Ctrl+1 through Alt+Ctrl+9 keyboard shortcuts.
Navigation pane	The "Headings" list in the Navigation pane automatically uses the Heading 1-9 styles.
Outline view	The Heading 1-9 styles are automatically set to outline levels 1-9.
Save as .htm	The Heading 1-6 styles are automatically formatted using the h1-h6 tags.
Save as .pdf	You can automatically set up the pdf bookmarks to match the Heading 19 styles.
SEQ fields	The SEQ field can automatically continue or restart numbering based on the Heading 1-9 styles. Other styles cannot.
Table of contents	The Heading 1-9 styles are automatically set to TOC levels 1-9.

What is the best way to format text?

The best way to format text is to use a style. If you highlight text and format it using the buttons in the Home tab or the options in the Fonts or Paragraph dialog boxes, you are using manual (or "inline") formatting instead of a style.

Manual formatting is difficult to update or apply consistently. For example, if you want each heading to be red and bold, you could highlight each heading and manually make it bold and red. However, you might forget to make some of the headings red, or bold, or both. You might also decide to change the headings to underlined and blue. If you use manual formatting, you might be able to use the Find and Replace feature to update the formatting. Unfortunately, you will probably end up reformatting the headings manually.

If you use a style, you can apply multiple formatting options at the same time. You won't need to worry about selecting the correct shade of red or the correct font. If you decide to change any of the formatting options, all of the content that uses the style will be immediately updated when you modify and save the style changes.

For more information about using styles, see the "Styles and themes" chapter on page 331.

How do I add borders?

You can add borders using a style. However, you can also use the following keyboard shortcuts to add a border:

Shortcut	Result
Press - (hyphen) three times and press Enter	Underline border of ¾ points
Press _ (underscore) three times and press Enter	Underline border of 1½ points
Press ~ (tilde) three times and press Enter	Zigzag underline border
Press * (asterisk) three times and press Enter	Dotted underline border

Shortcut	Result
Press = (equal to) three times and press Enter	Double underline border

How do I change the default font?

If you prefer a specific font, you can make it the default font for new documents.

To change Word's default font:

1 Press **Ctrl+Shift+F**.
The Font dialog box appears.

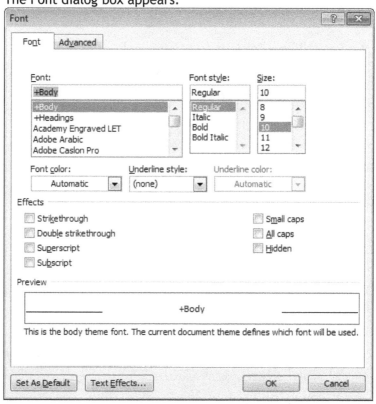

2 Select a **Font**.

3 Select a **Size**.

4 Click **Set as Default**.

5 Select **All documents based on the Normal.dotx template.**

6 Click **OK.**

How do I select a font when creating a Web page?

When you create a Web page, you should use fonts that your users also have on their computer, tablet, or phone. If you use a font they don't have, the font you used will be replaced with another font.

To select a font for a Web page:

1 Select **File > Options.**
The Word Options dialog box appears.

2 Select the **Advanced** tab.

3 Scroll down to the **General** section.

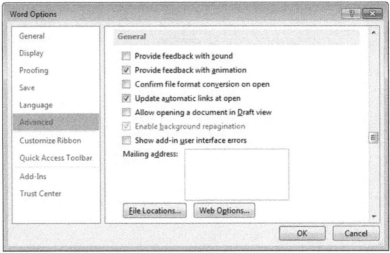

4 Click **Web Options.**
The Web Options dialog box appears.

5 Select the **Fonts** tab.

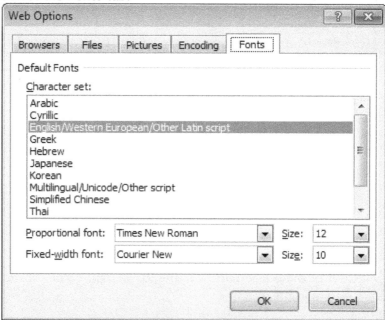

6 For **Proportional Font**, select the font you want to use as the default for your Web pages.

7 Select a **Size** for the proportional (default) text.

8 For **Fixed-width Font**, select the font you want to use for mono-spaced text.

9 Select a **Size** for the fix-width text.

10 Click **OK** to close the Web Options dialog box.

11 Click **OK** to close the Options dialog box.

How do I create a hanging indent?

You can use a hanging indent to indent all of the lines of a paragraph after the first line. Hanging indents are often used in bibliographies and "Works cited" references.

You can use the following keyboard shortcuts to create a hanging indent:

- create a hanging indent   **Ctrl+T**
- reduce a hanging indent   **Ctrl+Shift+T**

If you need to specify the indentation amount, you can use the Indents and Spacing dialog box.

To create a hanging indent:

1 Select the paragraph you'd like to format.

2 Select the **Home** tab.
—OR—
Press **Alt+H**.

3 Click the ⌐ small arrow in the lower-right corner of the **Paragraph** group.

4 Select the **Indents and Spacing** tab.

5 For **Special**, select **Hanging**.

6 For **By**, select how far the content should be indented.

7 Click **OK**.

How do I align paragraphs?

You can use the following keyboard shortcuts to align paragraphs:

Shortcut	Result
Ctrl+M	Indent a paragraph from the left
Ctrl+Shift+M	Remove a left indent
Ctrl+L	Left align a paragraph
Ctrl+E	Switch between centered and left-aligned
Ctrl+R	Switch between right-aligned and left-aligned
Ctrl+J	Switch between justified and left-aligned

How do I apply the "Normal" style?

You can press **Ctrl+Shift+N** to apply the "Normal" paragraph style.

How do I copy and paste formatting?

You can use the Format Painter to copy the formatting applied to one block of text and paste it to other blocks of text.

To use the Format Painter:

1 Select the text that has the formatting you wish to copy. If the formatting you wish to copy includes bullets, numbering, indents, borders, shading, or changes in alignment or spacing, select the entire paragraph, including the ¶ at the end of the paragraph.

2   Select the **Home** tab.
—OR—
Press **Alt+H**.

3   Click the **Format Painter** button in the **Clipboard** group.

🖌 Format Painter

4   Select the text to which you wish to apply the formatting.

TIP▶ *Double-click **Format Painter** to enable the feature indefinitely. Then, you can apply the formatting to multiple blocks of text. When you are done, click **Format Painter** again or press **Esc**.*

To copy and paste formatting using the keyboard:

1   Select the text whose format you want to copy.

2   Press **Shift+Ctrl+C**.
The formatting is copied.

3   Select the text you want to format.

4   Press **Shift+Ctrl+V**.
The formatting is applied.

Why does my formatting change when I paste content into other documents?

When you copy and paste content between documents, inline formatting will remain the same. For example, if you applied inline formatting to make a word bold, the word will remain bold. However, if you applied a style such as "Heading 1" that makes text bold, the text may not be bold when you paste it into another document. The reason is that the "Heading 1" style may not be defined as bold in the other document. The text will still be formatted as "Heading 1," and it will be formatted however the Heading 1 style is set up in the other document.

A theme can also change a document's formatting. If the second document uses a different theme, the formatting may change to match the theme.

If you want to remove formatting when pasting into a document:

1   Select the **Home** tab.
    —OR—
    Press **Alt+H**.

2   Click the **Copy** button in the **Clipboard** group.
    —OR—
    Press **Ctrl+C**.

3   Click the arrow for the **Paste** button in the **Clipboard** group.

4   Select **Paste Special**.

5   Select **Unformatted Text** or **Unformatted Unicode Text**.
    The text is pasted into the document without its formatting.

How do I remove inline paragraph formatting?

You can click the **Clear Formatting** button in the **Font** group to remove all inline formatting and change a paragraph's style to Normal.

How do I remove all formatting?

If you want to remove all of the formatting in a document, you will need to remove any inline formatting, remove any highlighting, and change all of the text to the "Normal" style.

To remove inline formatting:

1 Select the text.
   To select all of the text in a document, press **Ctrl+A**.

2 Select the **Home** tab.
   —OR—
   Press **Alt+H**.

3 Click the **Clear Formatting** button in the **Font** group.

To remove highlighting:

1 Select the text.
   To select all of the text in a document, press **Ctrl+A**.

2 Select the **Home** tab.
   —OR—
   Press **Alt+H**.

3 Click the **Text Highlight Color** button's drop-down arrow.

4 Select **No Color**.

To change all of the text to the "Normal" style:

1 Press **Ctrl+A** to select all of the text in the document.

2 Press **Ctrl+Shift+N**.

How do I adjust letter spacing?

You can adjust the letter spacing to make a heading fit on one line or to fine-tune the spacing for fully-justified paragraphs.

To adjust letter spacing:

1 Click inside a paragraph.

2 Press **Ctrl+D**.
   —OR—
   Click the ⌐ small arrow in the lower-right corner of the **Font** group.
   The Font dialog box appears.

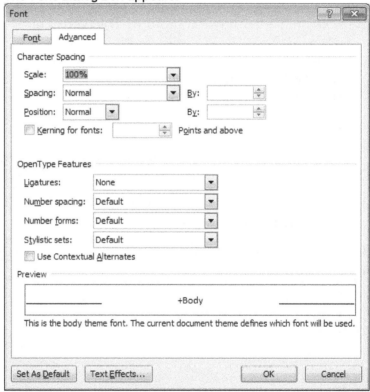

3 Set the **Scale** to the desired letter width.

4 If you also want to change the letter spacing, set the **Spacing** option.

5 Click **OK**.

How do I adjust line spacing?

Line spacing is the amount of spacing between each line. You can adjust the line spacing to single-, 1.5-, or double-spacing, or you can specify your own custom amount of spacing.

TIP *If you set the line spacing using a style, the spacing will be automatically applied when you use the style.*

To set the line spacing using a style (recommended):

1 Select the **Home** tab.
   —OR—
   Press **Alt+H.**

2 Click the ⌐ small arrow in the lower-right corner of the **Styles** group.
   —OR—
   Press **Shift+Ctrl+Alt+S.**
   The Styles task pane appears.

3 Hover the mouse over a styles in the list of styles.

4 Click the arrow to the right of the style's name and select **Modify**.

5 Click **Format** and select **Paragraph**.
   The Paragraph dialog box appears.

6 Select the **Indents and Spacing** tab.

7 In the **Spacing** section, select a **Line Spacing** amount and click **OK.**

8 Click **OK.**

To set the line spacing using inline formatting:

For this amount of spacing...	Press...
Single	**Ctrl+1**
1.5	**Ctrl+5**
Double	**Ctrl+2**

How do I set the paragraph spacing?

You can set the spacing before and after paragraphs. Unlike line spacing, paragraph spacing is added above or below the entire paragraph and not between each line.

If you set the paragraph spacing using a style, the spacing will be automatically applied when you use the style. In addition, you can modify the style to update any paragraphs that use the style.

To set the paragraph spacing using a style (recommended):

1 Select the **Home** tab.
 —OR—
 Press **Alt+H**.

2 Click the ⌐ small arrow in the lower-right corner of the **Styles** group.
 —OR—
 Press **Shift+Ctrl+Alt+S**.
 The Styles task pane appears.

3 Hover the mouse over a style in the list of styles.

4 Click the arrow to the right of the style's name and select **Modify**.

5 Click **Format** and select **Paragraph**.
 The Paragraph dialog box appears.

6 Select the **Indents and Spacing** tab.

7 In the **Spacing** section, select or type a **Before** and **After** spacing amount and click **OK**.

8 Click **OK**.

To set the paragraph spacing with inline formatting:

1 Click inside the paragraph you want to modify.

2 Click the ⌐ small arrow in the lower-right corner of the **Paragraph** group.

The Paragraph dialog box appears.

3 In the **Spacing** section, select or type a **Before** and **After**
   spacing amount.

4 Click **OK**.

How do I 'fix' full justification?

If you use full justification, Word will adjust the spacing
between words to fully align the content between the left and
right margin. This approach oftens adds too much space, as you
can see in this paragraph.

You can set the justification feature to work like WordPerfect, which does not add as much space between words.

To adjust the full justification setting:

1 Select **File** > **Options**.
The Word Options dialog box appears.

2 Select the **Advanced** tab.

3 Scroll down to the **Compatibility options** section.

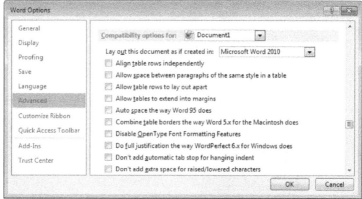

4 Select **Do full justification the way WordPerfect 6.x for Windows does.**

5 Click **OK**.

How do I vertically justify content?

You can vertically justify content to add a small amount of space between paragraphs and make the margins at the bottom of the page even.

To vertically justify content:

1 Select the **Page Layout** tab.
—OR—
Press **Alt+P**.

2 Click the ⌐ small arrow in the lower-right corner of the **Page Setup** group.

The Page Setup dialog box appears.

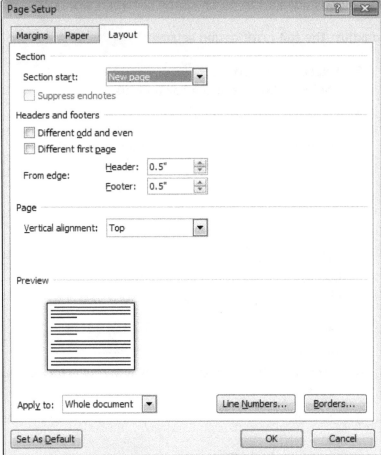

3   Select the **Layout** tab.

4   Select **Justified** in the **Vertical alignment** drop-down list.

5   Select **Whole document** in the **Apply to** list.

6   Click **OK**.
     Word repaginates the document and adjusts the space between
     paragraphs to fill pages to the bottom margin.

If the last page of the document is not a full page, Word will
spread the text out to the bottom of the page.

To turn off vertical justification on the last page:

1 Position the cursor at the top of the last page.

2 Press **Ctrl+Shift+Z** to select all of the text on the page.

3 Select the **Page Layout** tab.
   —OR—
   Press **Alt+P**.

4 Click the ⌐ small arrow in the lower-right corner of the **Page Setup** group.
   The Page Setup dialog box appears.

5 Select the **Layout** tab.

6 In the **Page** section, set the **Vertical alignment** to **Top**.

7 Click **OK**.
   Word will insert an section break and align the last page correctly.

Why does my formatting sometimes disappear when I apply a style?

If you click the buttons in the Font or Paragraph groups on the Home tab (or use their keyboard shortcuts), Word will use inline formatting. Ideally, you should use styles instead of inline formatting. Styles are much easier to maintain and update, and they ensure consistency throughout your document.

If you apply a style to a paragraph and less than half the text in the paragraph has inline formatting, Word will retain the inline formatting. If you apply a style to a paragraph and more than half of the text has inline formatting, the inline formatting will be removed.

How do I apply a text effect?

You can use the Text Effect feature to add outlines, shadows, and reflections to text.

To apply a text effect:

1   Select the text to which you wish to apply the effect.

2   Select the **Home** tab.
     —OR—
     Press **Alt+H**.

3   Click the [A ▾] **Text Effect** button in the **Font** group.

4   Select a text effect, or click **Outline**, **Shadow**, **Reflection** or **Glow** to create a custom effect.

How do I embed fonts in a document?

If you share a document with other writers or send it to someone to read, they will need to have the fonts you used on their computer. Otherwise, Word will substitute the font. The new font will change your layout, and, worst case, it could make your document unreadable.

To avoid font substitution, you can embed a font into a document. The font must be a TrueType font, and it must be available for embedding by the font designer.

To determine if a font is a TrueType font:

1   Select the **Home** tab.
     —OR—
     Press **Alt+H**.

2   Click the down arrow for the **Font** drop-down list in the **Fonts** group.
     TrueType fonts will have a Tт icon.

Fonts are set to one of four embedding compatibility levels:

- **Installable** – can be embedded and installed on other users' computers
- **Editable** - the document is editable in the embedded font, but the font cannot be installed on other users' computers
- **Print and preview** - The document will print with the correct font on other users' computers, but it is not editable and the font cannot be installed
- **Not embeddable** - the font cannot be embedded

To determine a font's embedding capability level, you can download Microsoft's free Font Properties Extension at:

http://goo.gl/rtjan

This application allows Windows to displays more information when you right-click a font select **Properties**. One of the tabs displayed in the Properties dialog box includes the font's embedding compatibility level.

To embed fonts in a document:

1 Select **File** > **Options**.
The Word Options dialog box appears.

2 Select the **Save** tab.

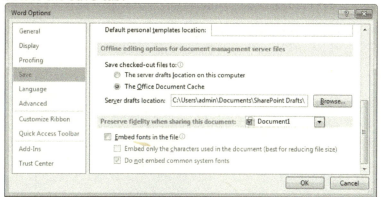

3 Select **Embed fonts in the file**.

4 If needed, check the following check boxes:

□ **Embed only the characters used in the document (best for reducing file size)** - if you are only distributing your document for viewing and not editing, select this option to decrease the file size.

□ **Do not embed common system fonts** - this option prevents the embedding of common Windows fonts, which decreases file size. If the fonts do not look correct for your users, uncheck this check box.

5   Click **OK**.

6   Re-save your document to embed the fonts.

◇ *If you embed fonts, your document's size increases by the size of the embedded fonts.*

How do I use OpenType font features?

If you use an OpenType font, you can specify advanced options such as how ligatures appear and how numbers are spaced.

To set OpenType features:

1   Select all or part of your document.

2   Press **Ctrl+D**.
    The Font dialog box appears.

3   Select the **Advanced** tab.

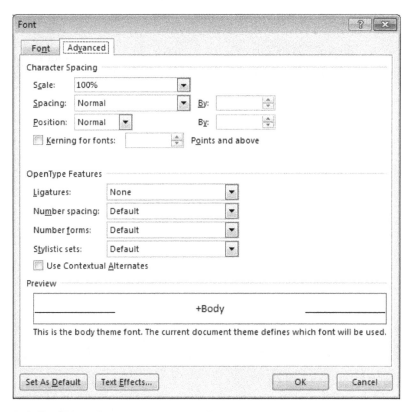

4 Set the **OpenType Features** options.

5 Click **OK**.

How do I create a cover page?

You can create a cover page for your document, such as a cover for a fax, report, or technical guide.

To create a cover page:

1 Select the **Insert** tab.
—OR—
Press **Alt+N**.

2 Click the **Cover Page** button in the **Pages** group.

3 Select a cover page.

4 Modify the cover page as desired.

5 Double-click inside the text fields to type document information such as the title and subtitle.

To remove a cover page:

1 Select the **Insert** tab.
—OR—
Press **Alt+N.**

2 Click the **Cover Page** button in the **Pages** group.

3 Select **Remove Current Cover Page.**

How do I apply a fill or gradient background?

You can apply a fill to add a background color (such as a yellow highlight) to your text. You can apply a gradient to add backgrounds that use a range of colors and/or effects such as reflections and glows.

To apply a gradient or fill:

1 Select the text you want to modify.

2 Select the **Home** tab.
—OR—
Press **Alt+H.**

3 Click the arrow beside the ⬛ Font Color button and select a color.

4 To apply a gradient:

☐ Click the arrow beside the ⬛ Font Color button again and select **Gradient.**

☐ Click a gradient style. To create a custom gradient, click **More Gradients** and select the text effect options you want to use.

How do I set a background color?

You can specify a background color for your document to make the content easier to read or if you plan to create a Web page.

To set the background color:

1 Select the **Design** tab.
   —OR—
   Press **Alt+D**.

2 Click the **Page Color** button in the **Page Background** group.

A small palette appears.

3 Select the color you want to use for the background of your documents.

⬦ *The background color is only visible if you are using the Print Layout or Web Layout view.*

How do I set the underlining color and style?

You can specify an underline color and style, including double, dotted, dashed, and wavy underlining.

To select underlining options:

1 Select the text you wish to underline.

2 Select the **Home** tab.

    —OR—

    Press **Alt+H**.

3 Click the ⌐ small arrow in the lower-right corner of the **Font** group.

    —OR—

    Press **Ctrl+D**.

    The Font dialog box appears.

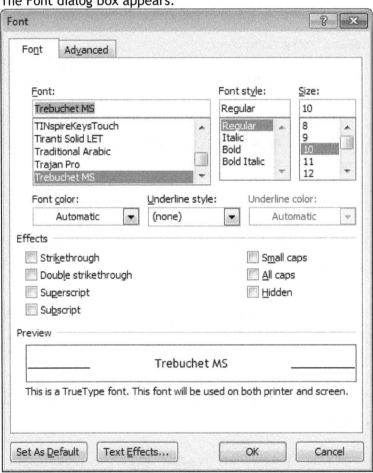

4 Select an **Underline style**.

5 Select an **Underline color**.

6 Click **OK**.

How do I create drop cap?

You can add drop caps to customize your text. Drop caps are often used in books for the first letter in a chapter.

> S o, also hierher kommen
> die Leute, um zu
> leben, ich würde eher
> meinen, es stürbe sich hier.

To create a drop cap:

1   Move your cursor to the start of a paragraph where you want the drop cap or initial cap to appear.

2   Select the **Insert** tab.
    —OR—
    Press **Alt+N**.

3   Click the **Drop Cap** button in the **Text** group.

4   Select one of the following options:

    ☐   None

    ☐   Dropped (standard Drop Cap)

    ☐   In margin (the letter moves to the left of the paragraph)

5   Format the drop cap.

How do I remove inline formatting?

You can remove inline formatting by highlighting the content and pressing **Ctrl+Space**. If you want to remove all of the inline formatting in a document, you can highlight the entire document by pressing **Ctrl+A**.

Are there different types of styles?

There are two types of styles: character styles and paragraph styles.

Character styles are used to format words and phrases. They appear in the Styles list with an a icon.

To apply a character style, highlight the content and select a style from the Styles list.

Paragraph styles are applied to all of the words in a paragraph, list item or table cell. They appear in the Styles list with a ¶ ("pilcrow") icon. Paragraph styles include "Normal" and "Heading 1."

To apply a paragraph style, click anywhere inside a paragraph and select the style from the Styles list.

How do I rotate text?

If your text is inside a shape, text box, or table cell, you can rotate it 90 degrees clockwise or counterclockwise.

To rotate text:

1   Select the shape, text box, or table cell that contains the text whose orientation you want to change.

2   Select the **Format** tab.

3   Click the **Text Direction** button in the **Alignment** group.

Each time you click **Text Direction**, the text will rotate another 90 degrees.

How do I change between single and double space after period?

You can set Word to mark single or double spacing as incorrect to help you find inconsistent spacing when writing. You can use the Replace feature to change between single and double spacing.

To mark single and double spacing as incorrect:

1 Select **File** > **Options**.
The Word Options dialog box appears.

2 Select the **Proofing** tab.

3 Scroll down to the **Writing Style** option.

4 Click **Settings**.
The Grammar Settings dialog box appears.

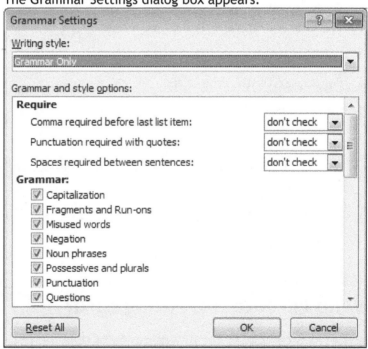

5 Set the **Spaces Required Between Sentences** option to the number of spaces you prefer between sentences.

6 Click **OK** to close the Grammar Settings dialog box.

7 Click **OK** to close the Word Options dialog box.

The grammar checker will mark incorrect spacing with a green wavy underline.

To change double spacing to single spacing:

1 Press **Ctrl+H**.

The Find and Replace dialog box appears.

2 For **Find what**, type a period followed by one space.

3 For **Replace with**, type a period followed by two spaces.

4 Click **Replace All**.

To change single spacing to double spacing:

1 Press **Ctrl+H**.

The Find and Replace dialog box appears.

2 For **Find what**, type . ^?

3 For **Replace with**, type . ^&

4 Click **Replace All**.

5 Perform another replace all:

- For **Find what**, type . . (period, space, period, and two spaces)

- For **Replace with**, type . (a period and two spaces)

- Click **Replace All**.

How do I create a greeting card?

Word provides templates for a wide range of documents, including greeting cards.

To create a greeting card:

1 Select **File** > **New**.

2 Click a document type.

3 Click **Create**.
   The new document will appear using the template you selected. If this is the first time you have used the template, Word will need to download the template from the Web.

How do I create a booklet or brochure?

You can set up a double-sided booklet or brochure with a gutter between the pages so you can fold the booklet or brochure after printing.

To create a booklet:

1 Select the **Page Layout** tab.
   —OR—
   Press **Alt+P**.

2 Click the ⌐ small arrow in the lower-right corner of the **Page Setup** group.
   The Page Setup dialog box appears.

3 Select the **Margins** tab.

4   In the **Margins** section, set amount of **Gutter** space.
    The gutter is where the document will be folded.

5   Set the **Orientation** to **Landscape**.

6   In the **Pages** section, set **Multiple Pages** to **Book fold**.

7   Select the number of **Sheets per booklet**.

8   Click **OK**.

How do I format a fraction?

When you type a commonly-used fraction, such as ½, Word will
automatically convert it to a single character fraction symbol.
However, less common fractions, such as 1/5 are not

automatically converted. You can use the superscript and subscript features to format less common fractions.

To format less common fractions:

1 Type your fraction.

2 Select the **Home** tab.
   —OR—
   Press **Alt+H**.

3 Select the numerator (the part to the left of the slash) and click the x^2 **Superscript** button in the **Font** group.

4 Select the denominator (the part to the right of the slash) and click the x_2 **Subscript** button in the **Font** group.

How do I find an RGB color?

You can find the RGB (red, green, blue) values of a color that is used in your document.

To find the RGB color value using the Font dialog box:

1 Select the text whose color you want examine.

2 Select the **Home** tab.
   —OR—
   Press **Alt+H**.

3 Click the ◲ small arrow in the lower-right corner of the **Font** group.
   A palette of colors appears.

4 Click **More Colors**.
   The Colors dialog box appears.

5 Select the **Custom** tab.

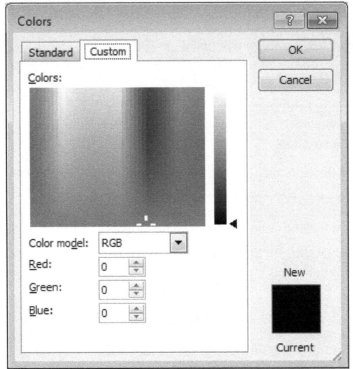

The RGB values appear at the bottom of the dialog box.

How do I add space between a border and text?

If you apply borders to a table, text, or other content, you can add space between the content and the border.

To add space between content and its border:

1 Select the text you want to change.
If you only need to format one paragraph, you can click inside the paragraph.

2 Select the **Home** tab.
—OR—
Press **Alt+H**.

3 Click the arrow for the [⬚ ▾] **Borders** button in the **Paragraph** group.

4 Select **Borders and Shading**.
The Borders and Shading dialog box appears.

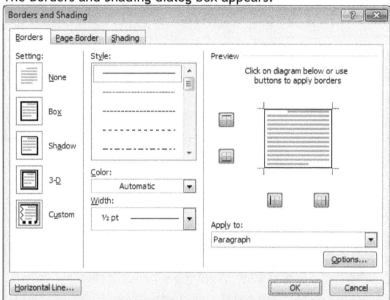

5 Click **Options**.
The Border and Shading Options dialog box appears.

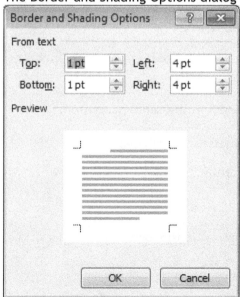

6 Set the **Top**, **Bottom**, **Left**, and **Right** spacing options.

7 Click **OK**.

How do I align numbers with decimals?

You can add a decimal tab stop to align numbers with decimals, such as currency values.

To align numbers with decimals:

1 Highlight the cells or paragraphs that contain the numbers you want to align.

2 Click the tab stop marker in the left ruler, and keep clicking until the symbol changes to ⬚.

3 Click the ruler where you want to align the numbers. A decimal tab stop is added to the ruler.

4 Press **Tab** to align the number by its decimal.

How do I left-, center-, and right-align content on same line?

You can use tabs to left-, right-, and even center-align content in the same paragraph.

To apply multiple alignments in the same paragraph:

1 Format the paragraph as left-aligned.

2 Select the **Home** tab.
—OR—
Press **Alt+H**.

3 Click the ⬚ small arrow in the lower-right corner of the **Paragraph** group.
The Paragraph dialog box appears.

4 Click **Tabs.**

The Tabs dialog box appears.

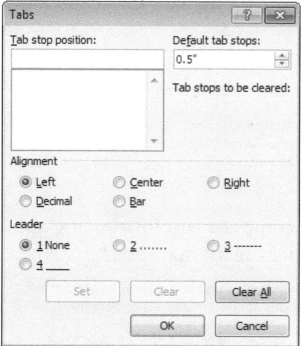

5 Type a **Default tab stop** position.

6 In the **Alignment** section, select an option.

7 Click **Set.**

8 Repeat steps 5-7 to add additional tab stops.

9 Click **OK.**

10 Type your text.

11 Press **Tab** to move to the next tab stop.

This approach works well if you are formatting a single line. If you are formatting multiple lines, it is usually easier to use a table with two or three columns.

How do I view the formatting applied to a word or paragraph?

You can use the Reveal Formatting pane to view a list of the formatting options applied to a word or paragraph.

To view the formatting applied to a word or paragraph:

- □ Press **Shift+F1**.
  The Reveal Formatting pane appears at the right side of the document.

How do I compare the formatting applied to two words or paragraphs?

You can use the Reveal Formatting pane to compare the formatting options applied to a word or paragraph.

To compare the formatting options applied to two words or paragraphs:

1 Highlight a word or paragraph.

2 Press **Shift+F1**.
  The Reveal Formatting pane appears.

3 Select the Compare to another selection check box.

4 Highlight another word or paragraph.

How do I specify the default formatting for new documents?

You can save your selected theme and style set, including any customizations you've made, as the default formatting for new documents.

To specify the default formatting for new documents:

1 Select the **Design** tab.
  —OR—
  Press **Alt+D.**

2 Select a theme.

3 Select a style set.

4 Customize the design as needed.

5 Click **Set as Default.**

6 Click **Yes.**

Forms

How do I insert a "Legacy" form control?

There are three types of controls:

- ☐ Legacy controls — these controls require a document to be protected to forms, which locks the document so that only the form controls can be edited.

- ☐ ActiveX controls — these controls are designed for Web pages, but they can work in other types of documents. They require macros.

- ☐ Content controls — these controls do not require form protection or macros.

Word 2013 groups the form and ActiveX controls together as "Legacy" form controls.

To insert a Legacy form control:

1 Position the cursor where you want to insert the control.

2 Select the **Developer** tab.
—OR—
Press **Alt+L.**

3 Click the ▦▾ **Legacy Tools** button in the **Controls** group.

4 Click a control in the list.

How do I insert a text control?

You can insert a Rich Text or Plain Text control to allow other users to type content into a document. A Rich Text control can be formatted.

To insert a text control:

1   Position the cursor where you want to insert the text control.

2   Select the **Developer** tab.
    —OR—
    Press **Alt+L.**

3   To insert a formatted text control, click the Aa **Rich Text Content Control** button in the **Controls** group.
    To insert a plain text control, click the Aa **Plain Text Content Control** button in the **Controls** group.

4   Type the text inside the control.

5   If you inserted a Rich Text control, format the text as desired.

How do I insert a date picker control?

You can insert a Date Picker control to allow users to select a date from a calendar.

To insert a Date Picker control:

1   Position the cursor where you want to insert the date picker control.

2   Select the **Developer** tab.
    —OR—
    Press **Alt+L.**

3   Click the ▦ **Date Picker Content Control** button in the **Controls** group.
    The date control appears in the document.

4   Click the drop-down arrow and select a date.

How do I insert a check box?

You can insert a check box to allow users to select multiple items in a group. For example:

Which type of vehicle do you own (select all that apply):

☐ Car

☐ Truck

☐ Van

☐ Motorcyle

To insert a check box:

1 Position the cursor where you want to insert the check box.

2 Select the **Developer** tab.
   —OR—
   Press **Alt+L.**

3 Click the ☑ **Check Box Content Control** button in the **Controls** group.
   The check box control appears in the document.

How do I insert a combo box or drop-down list?

You can insert a combo box or drop-down box to allow the user to select an item from a list. A combo box allows the user to type or select a value, but a drop-down only allows the user to select an item from a list.

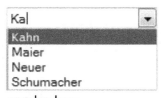

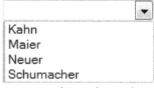

combo box   drop-down box

To insert a combo box or drop-down list:

1 Position the cursor where you want to insert the combo box or drop-down list.

2 Select the **Developer** tab.
   —OR—
   Press **Alt+L**.

3 Click the ▤ **Combo Box Content Control** or ▤ **Drop-Down List Control** button in the **Controls** group.
   The control appears in the document.

4 Click inside the combo box or drop-down list.

5 Select **Properties** in the **Controls** group.

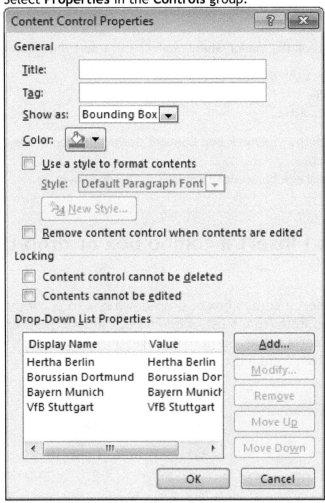

6 Type a **Title**.

7 For each item in the list:

- □ Click **Add.**

- □ Type a **Display Name.**

- □ Type a **Value.**

- □ Click **OK.**

8   Click **OK.**

How do I protect a document?

You protect a document so that users can only use selected styles or edit specified sections.

To protect a document.

1   Select the **Developer** tab.
    —OR—
    Press **Alt+L.**

2   Click the **Restrict Editing** button in the **Protect** group.

Restrict
Editing

The Restrict Editing Pane appears.

3   To protect a document's formatting:

- □ Select the **Limit formatting to a selection of styles** check box.

- □ Click **Settings.**

- □ Select the styles that will be available for use in the document.

- □ Select whether autoformatting should be allowed to override styles.

- □ Select whether you want to **Block Theme or Scheme switching.**

- □ Select whether you want to **Block Quick Style Set switching.**

- □ Click **OK.**

4 Select the **Editing restrictions** you want to apply.

5 To prevent users from editing a document:

- □ Select the **Allow only this type of editing in the document** check box.

- □ Select the type of editing that is allowed.

- □ Highlight any content you want to allow specified users to edit.

- □ Select the user's checkbox.
  You can click **More users** to add additional users.

6 Click **Yes, Start Enforcing Protection.**

Headers and footers

How do I create a different first page header and footer?

You can create different headers and footers for the first page in a document or section. Many users create a blank header and footer for the first page in a document, since it's often a title page.

To create different first page headers and footers:

1   Select the **Page Layout** tab.
    —OR—
    Press **Alt+P**.

2   Click the ⌐ small arrow in the lower-right corner of the **Page Setup** tab.

The Page Setup dialog box appears.

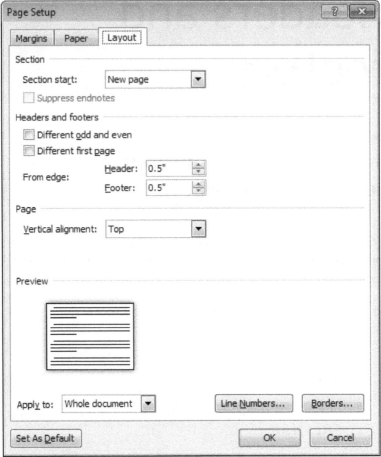

3 Select the Layout tab.

4 In the **Headers and Footers** section, select the **Different first page** check box.

5 Click **OK**.

How do I create different odd and even headers and footers?

You can create different headers and footers for odd and even pages. For example, many users left-align the header and/or footer on even (left) pages and right-align them on odd (right) pages.

To create different odd and even headers and footers:

1 Select the **Page Layout** tab.
  —OR—
  Press **Alt+P**.

2 Click the ⌐ small arrow in the lower-right corner of the **Page Setup** tab.
  The Page Setup dialog box appears.

3 Select the **Layout** tab.

4 In the **Headers and Footers** section, select the **Different odd and even** check box.

5 Click **OK**.

How do I add content to the header or footer?

You can add any type of content to a document's header or footer, including text, tables, and pictures.

To add content to the header or footer:

1 Select the **Insert** tab.
  —OR—
  Press **Alt+N**.

2 Click the **Header** or **Footer** button in the **Header & Footer** group.

3 Select **Edit Header** or **Edit Footer**.

4 If necessary, press **Tab** to move to the desired section of the header or footer.

5 In the **Insert** ribbon, click **Quick Parts** > **Field**. The Fields dialog box appears.

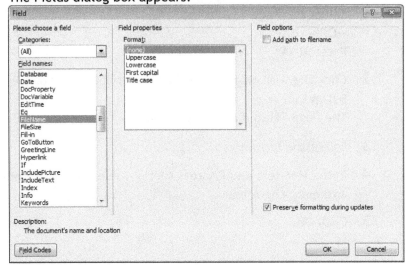

6 In the **Field names** list, select **FileName**.

7 For **Field Options**, select **Add path to filename**.

8 Click **OK**.

Index

Overview

You can create an index entry:

- for a word or phrase
- for a section or chapter that spans a range of pages
- that refers to another entry, such as "Vespa. See Piaggio"

When you select text and mark it as an index entry, Word adds a **XE** ("Index Entry") field.

How do I mark entries based on formatting or a style?

You can find all of the terms in a document that use a specific formatting option, such as boldfacing, or a specific style. If you copy and paste these terms into a new document, you can create an "automark" document and automatically create index entries.

To create an index based on formatting or a style:

1 Create a new, blank document.

2 Open your source document.

3 Press **Ctrl+H**.
   The Find and Replace dialog box appears with the Replace tab

selected.

4 Select the **Find** tab.

5 Clear the **Find what** box.

6 Click **More**.

7 Use the **Format** options to specify the formatting or style used for the index terms.

8 Click **Reading Highlight**.
Word highlights all the words in the document that use the specified format or style.

9 Press **Ctrl+C**.
All the words are copied to the clipboard.

10 Open to the blank document.

11 Press **Ctrl+V**.
The words are added to the document.

12 Select the **Home** tab.
—OR—
Press **Alt+H**.

13 Click the Sort button in the **Paragraph** group.

14 Search through the list and delete any duplicates.

15 Press **Ctrl+A**.

16 Select the **Insert** tab.

17 Click the **Table** button in the **Tables** group.

18 Select **Convert Text to Table**.

19 Click **OK**.

20 Right-click inside the table and select **Insert > Insert Right**.
A blank column appears.

21 In the second column, type how you want the term to appear in the index.
For example, you may want to use initial caps for the index. If you want the term to be the same, you can copy and paste it from the left column.

22 Save the list of terms document.
This document will be your automark term list.

To auto-mark terms:

1 Select the **References** tab.
—OR—
Press **Alt+S**.

2 Click the **Insert Index** button in the **Index** group.

The Index tab of the Index dialog box appears.

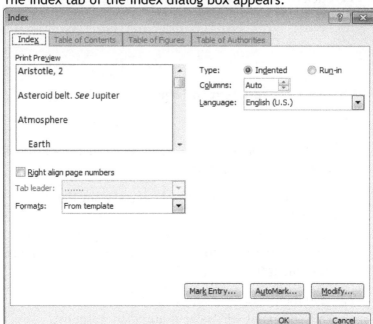

3 Click **AutoMark.**
The Open Index AutoMark File dialog box appears.

4 Select you automark terms document.

5 Click **Open.**

How do I mark index entries?

To mark index entries, do one of the following:

- □ Mark words or phrases
- □ Mark entries for text that spans a range of pages

To mark index entries:

1 To use existing text as an index entry, select the text.
To enter your own text as an index entry, click where you want
to insert the index entry.

2 Select the **References** tab.
  —OR—
  Press **Alt+S**.

3 Click the **Mark Entry** button in the **Index** group.

Mark
Entry

The Mark Entry dialog box appears.

4 Type or modify the main entry text.

5 If you are adding a subentry, type the subentry text.
  For example:
  Index,
    Marking entries 154

6 In the **Options** section, select **Current page**.

7 If the index entry's page number should be bold or italic, select
  the **Bold** and/or **Italic** check boxes.

8 Click **Mark.**
If you want to mark all of the text that matches the selected word or phrase, click **Mark All.**

To mark a range of pages, such as a chapter or section:

1 Select the range of text you want to mark.

2 Select the **Insert** tab.
—OR—
Press **Alt+N.**

3 Click the **Bookmark** button in the **Links** group.

4 Type a **Bookmark name.**

5 Click **Add.**

6 Position the cursor at the end of the text you bookmarked.

7 Select the **References** tab.
—OR—
Press **Alt+S.**

8 Click the **Mark Entry** button in the **Index** group.

9 The Mark Entry dialog box appears.

10 Type or modify the main entry text.

11 If you are adding a subentry, type the subentry text.
For example:
Index,
    Marking entries 154

12 In the **Options** section, select **Page range**.

13 If the index entry's page number should be bold or italic, select the **Bold** and/or **Italic** check boxes.

14 Click **Mark**.

How do I create an index?

Once you have marked your index terms, you can create an index. Word will find all of the XE ("Index Entry") fields in your document and create an alphabetical list of the markers and their corresponding page numbers.

To insert an index:

1 Position the insertion point where you want to insert the index.

2 Select the **References** tab.
—OR—
Press **Alt+S**.

3 Click the **Insert Index** button in the **Index** group.

The Index dialog box appears.

Index				? X

| Index | Table of Contents | Table of Figures | Table of Authorities |

Print Preview

Aristotle, 2

Asteroid belt. *See* Jupiter

Atmosphere

Earth

Type: ⦿ Indented ○ Run-in
Columns: Auto
Language: English (U.S.)

☐ Right align page numbers
Tab leader: ....
Formats: From template

Mark Entry...   AutoMark...   Modify...

OK   Cancel

4 Use the controls in the dialog box to indicate how you want the index to appear.

5 Click **OK**.

Labels

How do I print labels?

You can format a document to print on labels, such as DVD or file folder labels.

To create a label:

1   Select the **Mailings** tab.
     —OR—
     Press **Alt+M**.

2   Click the **Labels** button in the **Create** group.

     Labels

     The Envelopes and Labels dialog box appears.

3   Click **Options**.
     The Label Options dialog box appears.

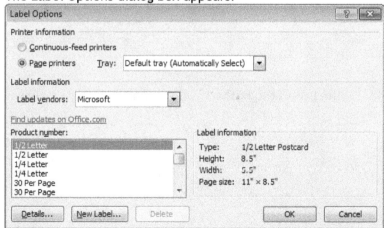

4   Select whether you are using a dot-matrix continuous feed printer or a "page" printer such as an inkjet or laser printer.

5   Select a **Label vendor**.

6 Select a **Product number.**

7 Click **OK.**

8 Click **New Document.**
The Envelopes and Labels dialog box appears.

9 If you do not see gridlines:

- □ Click **Design.**

- □ Click **Borders.**

- □ Click **View Gridlines.**

10 Type a label.

How do I create a return address label?

You can create and print return address labels for envelopes.

To create a return address label:

1 Select the **Mailings** tab.
—OR—
Press **Alt+M.**

2 Click the **Labels** button in the **Create** group.

The Labels tab of the Envelopes and Labels dialog box appears.

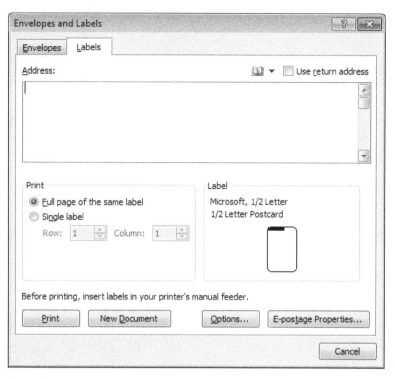

3 If you need to change the type of labels on which you are printing:

  □ Click **Options**.

  □ Select the options you want to use.

  □ Click **OK**.

4 Select the **Use Return Address** check box.
   Your return address should appear in the Address area of the dialog box.

5 If your return address does not appear:

  □ Select **File > Options**.
     The Word Options dialog box appears.

  □ Select the **Advanced** tab.

  □ Scroll down to the **General** section.

  □ In the **Mailing Address** area, type your return address.

  □ Click **OK**.

6 Print your labels.

How do I create a custom label?

You can create a custom label if you are designing your own labels or if you cannot find a pre-printed label to use.

To create a custom label:

1 Select the **Mailings** tab.
—OR—
Press **Alt+M**.

2 Click the **Labels** button in the **Create** group.

The Envelopes and Labels dialog box with the Labels tab selected.

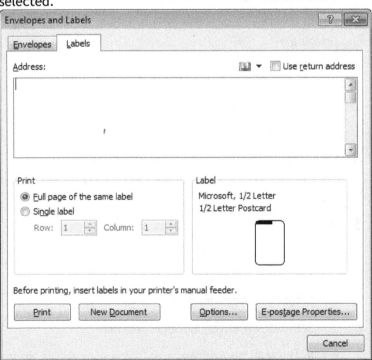

3   Click **Options**.

The Label Options dialog box appears.

4   Click New Label.

The Label Details dialog box appears.

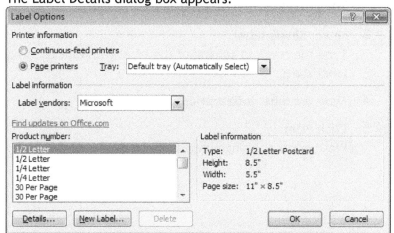

5   Select whether you are using a dot-matrix continuous feed printer or a "page" printer such as an inkjet or laser printer.

6   Select a **Label vendor**.

7   Select a **Product number**.

8   Click **OK**.

The name of your new label appears in the Product Number list.

9   Click **Print**.

How do I print one label?

Usually, the same labels is printed multiple times on a page. However, you can print one label if you don't need multiple labels.

To print one label:

1   Select the **Mailings** tab.

—OR—

Press **Alt+M**.

2 Click the **Labels** button in the **Create** group.

The Envelopes and Labels dialog box appears.

3 Select **Single label**.
Type the row and column of the label you want to use on the label sheet.

4 Type the **label information**.

5 Click **Print**.
Word prints the single label.

Layouts

How do I add a page or section break?

You can add the following types of breaks to a document:

- **Page breaks**— the text begins at the top of a new page.

- **Column breaks** — the text begins at the top of a new column (or a new page if you only have one column).

- **Section breaks** — the text begins at the top of a new section. Each section can have a different header and footer, margins, and page size.

- **Text-wrapping breaks** — the text begins on the next line. Text-wrapping breaks are used to wrap text around pictures.

To insert a break:

1 Position the insertion point where you want to insert the break.

2 Select the **Page Layout** tab.
   —OR—
   Press **Alt+P**.

3 Click the **Breaks** button in the **Page Setup** group.

4 Select a break type from the list.

How do I create columns?

You can add columns to a document to create a newsletter-, newspaper-, or magazine-style layout.

To format your content in columns:

1 Select the **Page Layout** tab.
   —OR—
   Press **Alt+P**.

2 Click the **Columns** button in the **Page Setup** group.

3 Select the number of columns you want to use
   —OR—
   Click **More Columns** to create a custom column layout.

If you only want part of your document to use columns, insert "Continuous" section breaks above and below the section you wish to display in columns.

How do I have a one-column heading with multi-column content?

You may want to divide a story or article across multiple columns with a headline that spans all the columns.

To create a heading that spans multiple columns:

1 Format your text so that it uses multiple columns:

   ☐ Select the content that should be formatted in columns.

   ☐ Select the **Page Layout** tab.
      —OR—
      Press **Alt+P**.

   ☐ Click the **Columns** button in the **Page Setup** group.

2 Type and select the heading.

3 Select the **Page Layout** tab.

4 Click the **Columns** button in the **Page Setup** group.

5 Select **More Columns**.
The Columns dialog box appears.

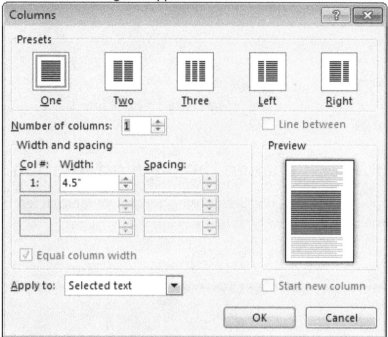

6 In the **Presets** section, select **One**.

7 For **Apply To**, select **Selected Text**.

8 Click **OK**.

How do I change the page size?

You can select a common paper size, such as 8.5x11" or A4, or you can specify another size if you are printing on custom-sized paper.

To change the paper size:

1 Select the **Page Layout** tab.
—OR—
Press **Alt+P**.

2 Click the **Size** button in the **Page Setup** group.

3 Select a paper size.
To select a custom size, select **More Paper Sizes**.

How do I change the page orientation?

You can design a document using portrait or landscape orientation.

To change the page orientation:

1 Select the **Page Layout** tab.
—OR—
Press **Alt+P**.

2 Click the **Orientation** button in the **Page Setup** group.

The current orientation appears highlighted.

3 Select an option.

How do I use portrait and landscape orientation in a document?

You can add section breaks to use portrait and landscape orientation in the same document.

To use portrait and landscape orientation in the same document:

1   Position the insertion point at the point where you want to change the orientation.

2   Select the **Page Layout** tab.
    —OR—
    Press **Alt+P.**

3   Click the **Breaks** button in the **Page Setup** group.

4   Select any of the **Section Break** options.

5   Move the insertion point to where you want to end the landscape or portrait orientation.

6   Insert the same type of section of break.

7   Position the insertion point anywhere between the two breaks.

8   Select the **Page Layout** tab.
    —OR—
    Press **Alt+P.**

9   Click the ⌐ small arrow in the lower-right corner of the **Page Setup** group.
    The Page Setup dialog box appears.

10 Select the **Margins** tab.

11 Select **Landscape** or Portrait orientation.

12 For **Apply to,** select **This Section.**

13 Click **OK.**

How do I set up mirror margins?

Mirror margins allow you to leave extra space for a book's binding. When you use mirror margins, you have "inside" (where the binding will be) and "outside" margins instead of left and right margins.

To set up mirror margins:

1 Select the **Page Layout** tab.

2 Click the **Margins** button in the **Page Setup** group.

3 Select **Mirrored**.

To change the page margins:

1 Click the **Margins** button in the **Page Setup** group.

2 Select **Custom Margins**.
The Page Setup dialog box appears.

3 Type or select a **Top, Bottom, Inside** or (**Left**) and **Outside** (or **Right**) margin.

4 Select a **Gutter position**.

5 Click **OK**.

How do I remove extra space above headings at top of the page?

If you have added space above a style, you can remove the extra space if the style is used at the top of a page. For example, you might add space above a "Heading 2" style so that it is separate from the paragraph above it. If a Heading 2 is at the top of a page, it doesn't need this extra space.

To remove extra space at the top of a page:

1 Select **File** > **Options**.
The Word Options dialog box appears.

2 Select the **Advanced** tab.

3 Scroll down to the **Compatibility Options** section.

4 If you want to apply the settings to all new documents, set the **Compatibility options for** option to **All New Documents**.

5 Set the **Lay out this document as if created** in option to **Microsoft Word 2010**.

6 Select **Suppress extra line spacing at top of page**.

7 Select **Suppress space before after a hard page or column break**.

8 Click **OK**.

How do I add pull quotes or sidebars?

You can use the Text Box feature to add pull quotes and sidebar to draw the reader's attention to content.

pull quote

sidebar

To create a pull quote or sidebar:

1 Select the **Insert** tab.
   —OR—
   Press **Alt+N**.

2 Select the page on which you want to place the pull quote or sidebar.

3 Click the **Text Box** button in the **Text** group.

A text box appears.

4 Click the text box.

5 Click the Wrap Text button.

6 Select a wrapping option.

7 If you want to rotate the text box, click the ⟳ rotate icon and move the mouse.

8 Click inside the text box and type the pull quote or sidebar.

How do I create flashcards?

You can create and print flashcards to help you study for a test or learn a language.

1   Select the **Page Layout** tab.
    —OR—
    Press **Alt+P**.

2   Click the **Size** button in the **Page Setup** group.

3   Select one of the index card sizes (3x5, 4x6, or 5x8).

4   Add your content to each page.

5   Print the cards.

Links

How do I create a hyperlink?

You can create a hyperlink to a document, such as a spreadsheet or presentation, or to a Web page.

1 Highlight the content that should be linked.

2 Select the **Insert** tab.
—OR—
Press **Alt+N**.

3 Click the **Hyperlink** button in the **Links** group.

4 To link to a document, select the document in the list.
To link to a Web page, type the Web page's address.

5 Click **OK**.
The hyperlink appears in your document.

How do I create a cross reference?

You can insert a cross reference to a heading, numbered item, footnote, endnote, equation, table, figure, or bookmark in a document.

To create a cross reference:

1 Position the insertion point where you want to insert the cross-reference.

2 Select the **Insert** tab.
—OR—
Press **Alt+N**.

3 Click the **Cross-reference** button in the **Links** group.

The Cross-reference dialog box appears.

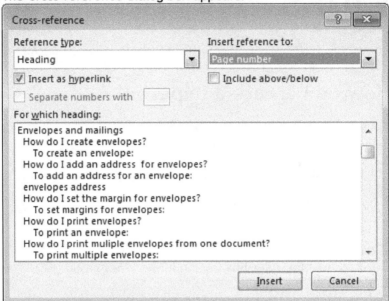

4 Select a **Reference type**.

5 Select whether you want the cross reference to display the page number, heading text, or heading number.

6 Select a reference, such as a heading.

7 Click **Insert**.

How do I create a bookmark?

Bookmarks are used to mark a location in a document. For example, you could add a bookmark before a heading, table, or picture. After you create a bookmark, you can create a link to it.

To create a bookmark:

1 Position the insertion point where you want to add the bookmark.

The location can be a word, the beginning of a paragraph, or a heading.

2 Select the **Insert** tab.
—OR—
Press **Alt+N**.

3 Click the **Bookmark** button in the **Links** group.

The Bookmark dialog box appears.

4 Type a name for the bookmark.
The bookmark name cannot contain spaces.

5 Click **Add**.

To find a bookmark:

1 Press **F5** or **Ctrl+G**.
The Find and Replace dialog box appears with the Go To tab

selected.

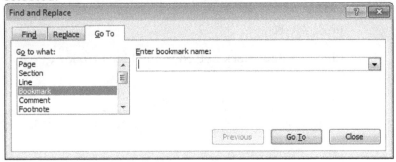

2   For **Go to what**, select **Bookmark**.

3   For **Enter bookmark name**, select a bookmark.

4   Click **Go To**.

5   Click **Close**.

How do I create a link to a bookmark?

You can create a link to a bookmark in a document, such as the first page in a chapter.

1   Highlight the content that should be linked.

2   Select the **Insert** tab.
    —OR—
    Press **Alt+N**.

3   Click the **Hyperlink** button in the **Links** group.

The Insert Hyperlink dialog box appears.

4 Select **Place in This Document**.

5 Select a **Bookmark**.

6 Click **OK**.
   The hyperlink appears in your document.

How do I change or remove link underlining?

By default, hyperlinks are blue and underlined.

You can change the color and remove the underlining by modifying the "Hyperlink" style.

To change hyperlink formatting:

1 Click inside a hyperlink.

2 Select the **Home** tab.
   —OR—
   Press **Alt+H**.

3 Click the ⌐ small arrow in the lower-right corner of the **Styles** group.

—OR—

Press **Shift+Ctrl+Alt+S.**

The Styles pane appears.

4 Hover the mouse pointer over the Hyperlink style.

5 Click the down arrow to the right of the Hyperlink style's name and select **Modify.**

The Modify Style dialog box appears.

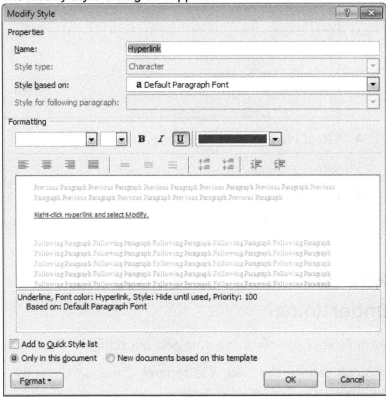

6 Click **Format.**

7 Select **Font**.

The Font dialog box appears.

8 Use the options to format hyperlinks.

9 Click **OK** to close the Font dialog box.

10 Click **OK** to close the Modify Style dialog box.

How do I turn off auto-linking?

By default, Word will automatically create a hyperlink when you type a URL, such as http://www.clickstart.net. You can turn off the auto-linking feature if you find it annoying.

To turn off auto-linking:

1 Select **File** > **Options**.
   The Word Options dialog box appears.

2 Select the **Proofing** tab.

3 In the **AutoCorrect** options, click **AutoCorrect Options**.
   The AutoCorrect dialog box appears.

4 Select the **AutoFormat** tab.

5 For **Replace**, uncheck **Internet and network paths with hyperlinks**.

6 Select the **AutoFormat As You Type** tab.

7 In **Replace as you type**, uncheck **Internet and network paths with hyperlinks**.

8 Click **OK**.

How do I stop links from auto-updating when I open a document?

Word will automatically check and update your links when you open a document. You can turn off this feature if you do not want your links to auto-update when you open a document.

To stop links from auto-updating:

1 Select **File** > **Options**.
   The Word Options dialog box appears.

2 Select the **Advanced** tab.

3 Scroll down to the **General** group.

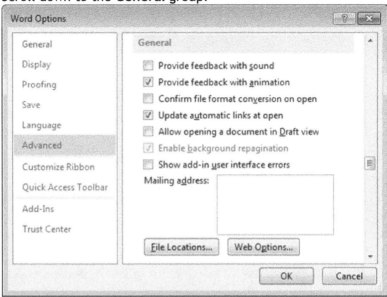

4 Select the **Update automatic links at open** check box.

5 Click **OK**.

This setting applies to your computer, not to the document. If someone else opens the document, they may still be asked to update the links.

How do I open a link by clicking it?

By default, you can open a link in a Word document pressing Ctrl and clicking the link. If you do not want to press Ctrl, you can set up Word to open links when they are clicked.

To open links when clicked (without pressing the Ctrl key):

1 Select **File > Options**.
The Word Options dialog box appears.

2 Select the **Advanced** tab.

3 Scroll to the **Editing options** section.

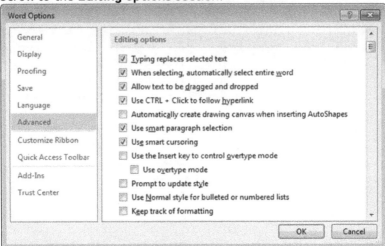

4 Uncheck the **Use CTRL+Click to follow hyperlink** check box.

5 Click **OK**.

You can now click links in your document without holding the Ctrl key.

Lists and numbers

How do I create a list?

You can create a bulleted or numbered list or even nested bulleted or numbered lists.

To create a list:

1   Type your list.

2   Select all of the items in the list.

3   Select the **Home** tab.
    —OR—
    Press **Alt+H**.

4   To create a numbered list, click the ![numbering icon] **Numbering** button in the **Paragraph** group.

    To create a bulleted list, click the ![bullets icon] **Bullets** button in the **Paragraph** group.

How do I format lists?

You can format the list number or bullet separately or together with the content of the list.

To format a list:

1   Click the ![pilcrow icon] **Show/Hide** button in the **Paragraph** group.

    TIP▶ *The "backwards P" symbol is called a pilcrow.*

2   Do one of the following:

    ☐   To format the list's content and bullet/number, select the entire list and the ¶.

- ❑ To format the list's content but not the bullet/number, select the list but do not select the ¶.

- ❑ To format the bullet/number but not the list's content, only select the ¶.

3 Select the **Home** tab.
—OR—
Press **Alt+H**.

4 Use the buttons in the Font group to format the selected content.

How do I convert bullets to numbers?

You can change a bulleted list to a numbered list or vice versa.

To change a list to bulleted or numbered:

1 Select the items in the list you want to convert.

2 Select the **Home** tab.
—OR—
Press **Alt+H**.

3 Do one of the following:

- ❑ To convert a bulleted list to a numbered list, click the **Numbering** button in the **Paragraph** group.

- ❑ To convert a numbered list to a bulleted list, click the **Bullets** button in the **Paragraph** group.

How do I convert a list to paragraphs?

You can convert a bulleted or numbered list to paragraphs.

To convert a list to a paragraph:

1   Highlight the list.

2   Click the ⬛ ▾ **Bullets** or ⬛ ▾ **Numbering** button in the
    Paragraph group.
    The list is converted to paragraphs.

How do I change the bullet marker?

Word provides numerous built-in bullet markers you can use. You
can also use a symbol or your own icon as a bullet marker.

To change the bullet marker:

1   Select the **Home** tab.
    —OR—
    Press **Alt+H**.

2   Click the down-arrow at the right of the ⬛ ▾ **Bullets** button
    in the **Paragraph** group.

3   Select a bullet style.

4   If you don't like any of the styles shown, click **Define New
    Bullet**.

The Define New Bullet dialog box appears.

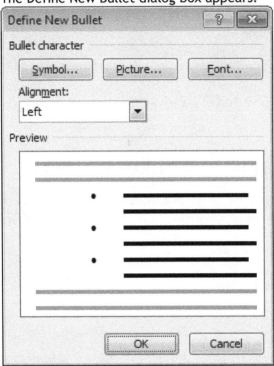

5 Click **Symbol**. If you want to use your own icon, click **Picture**.
The Symbol dialog box appears.

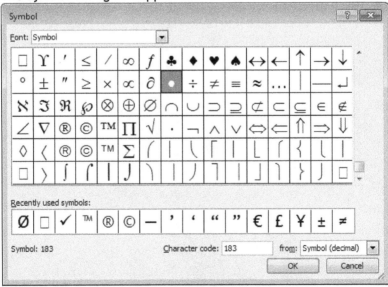

6 Select a symbol to use as a bullet. If you don't see the symbol you want to use, select a different **Font**.

7 Click **OK** to close the Symbol dialog box.

8 Click **OK** to close the Define New Bullet dialog box.

How do I number headings or captions?

If you use Word's built-in "Heading" 1-9 styles, you can use the Outline Numbering feature to add numbers.

To number headings using the built-in "Heading" styles:

1 Select the **Home** tab.
—OR—
Press **Alt+H**.

2 Click the [icon] **Multilevel list** button in the **Paragraph** group.

3 Select one of the numbering styles that includes the word "Heading" in the numbering scheme.

If you do not use Word's built-in Heading styles, or you need to number captions, you can create your own numbering style.

To create a numbering style:

1 Select the **Home** tab.
—OR—
Press **Alt+H**.

2 Click the [icon] **Multilevel list** button in the **Paragraph** group.

3 Select **Define New Multilevel List**.
The Define New Multilevel list dialog box appears.

4 Click **More.**

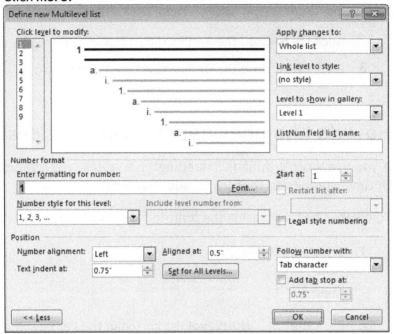

5 Select **1.**

6 For **Link level to style**, select the style you want to number. For example: "FigCaption"

7 Format the number as desired.

8 Click **OK.**

How do I number pages and chapters?

You can automatically include a chapter number as part of your page numbers. For example, your pages could be numbered as "1-1," "1-2," etc.

To include chapter numbers in your page numbers, you will need to use a style such as "Heading 1" for your chapter headings. Whenever you use this style, it will start a new chapter.

To number pages and chapters:

1 Select the **Insert** tab.
—OR—
Press **Alt+N**.

2 Click the **Page Number** button in the **Header & Footer** group.

3 Select **Format Page Number**.
The Page Number Format dialog box appears.

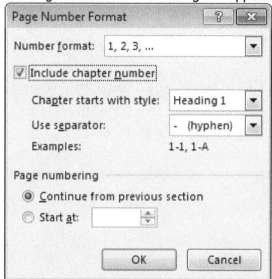

4 Select the **Include chapter number** check box.

5 Use the **Chapter starts with style** drop-down list to specify the style that will be used to begin each chapter.

6 For **Use Separator**, select a character to use between the chapter number and the page number.

7 Click **OK**.

How do I start numbering with 01?

You can use a **SEQ** field to add a 0 before your numbers. For example:

{SEQ Steps \# "0"}

◇ *You can also define a numbering format to add a 0, but it will not increment. When you reach 10, the number will become 010 instead of 10.*

To start numbering with a 0:

1   Press **Ctrl+F9**.
    The field code braces appear.

2   Inside the field code braces, type:
    SEQ Steps \# "0"

3   Press **Shift+F9** to replace the field codes with the field results.

Macros

How do I create a macro?

You can record a macro to perform a common task when you press a keyboard shortcut or click a button.

To create a macro:

1 Highlight some text in your document.

2 Select the **View** tab.
   −OR−
   Press **Alt+W**.

3 Click the arrow for the **Macros** button in the **Macros** group.

4 Select **Record Macro**.
   The Record Macro dialog box appears.

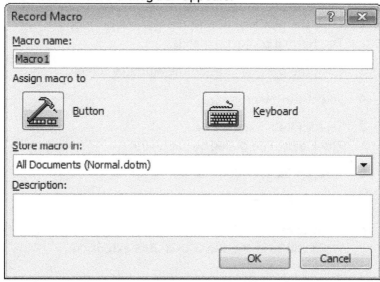

5 Type a **Macro name**.

◇ *A macro name can only contain letters and numbers.*

6 Click **Button**.
The Word Options dialog box appears.

7 Select the new macro's name in the list on the left.

8 Click **Add** to add the macro to your Quick Access Toolbar.

9 Click **OK**.
The cursor changes to a tape recorder.

10 Perform the tasks you want to record.

11 To stop recording, select **View** > **Macros** > **Stop recording**.
The macro is now ready for use.

How do I save or restore a macro?

You can save your macros to a file and share them with other Word users.

To save your macros to a file:

1 Press **Alt+F11**.
The Visual Basic Editor appears.

2 Click the plus sign beside the **Normal** project.
The Normal project expands.

3 Click the plus sign beside the **Modules** folder.

4 Select **NewMacros**.

5 Select **File** > **Export File**.
The Export File dialog box appears.

6 Select a location for the file.

7 Type a file name.

8 Click **Save**.
Word will save the file with a .BAS extension.

To import macros:

1 Press **Alt+F11**.
The Visual Basic Editor appears.

2 Select the **Normal** project.

3 Select **File** > **Import File.**
The Import File dialog box appears.

4 Select a .BAS file.

5 Click **Open**.

Merge

How do I use mail merge?

You can use mail merge to send a form letter to multiple recipients. You can either type the recipient list or select the recipients from a document or your email contact list.

To use mail merge to send a letter to multiple recipients:

1   Select the **Mailings** tab.
    —OR—
    Press **Alt+M**.

2   Click the **Start Mail Merge** button in the **Start Mail Merge** group.

Start Mail
Merge ▾

3   Select **Step-by-Step Mail Merge Wizard**.
    The Mail Merge pane appears.

4   Select the type of document you want to create.

5   Click **Next** at the bottom of the pane.

6   Select how you want to set up your document and click **Next**.

7   Select your recipients list and click **Next**.

8   Type your document.

9   Insert the recipients information as needed:

    ☐   To insert the recipient's name, click **More items**, select a name field, and click **Insert**.

□ To insert the recipient's address, click **Address block**, select a format, and click **OK**.

10 Click **Next**.

11 Preview your document and click **Next**.

12 To print the document, click **Print**.

How do I link to a page in another Word document?

You can create a link to a page in another Word document by adding a bookmark to the document.

To link to a page in a Word document:

1 Open both documents.
   We'll refer to the first document as "Doc1" and the second document as "Doc2."

2 In Doc2, position the insertion point at the beginning of the page to which you want to link.

3 Select the **Insert** tab.
   —OR—
   Press **Alt+N**.

4 Click the **Bookmark** button in the **Links** group.

The Bookmark dialog box appears.

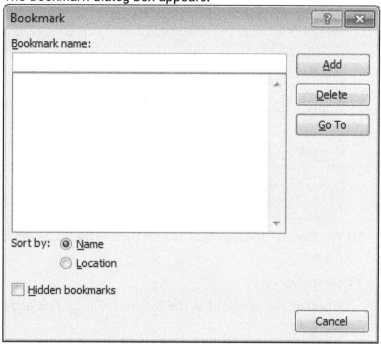

5 Type a **Bookmark name**, such as **MyBookmark**.

6 Click **Add**.
   The bookmark is added to the document.

7 Save Doc2.

8 In Doc1, position the insert point where you want the hyperlink
   to appear.

9 Press **Ctrl+K**.

The Insert Hyperlink dialog box appears.

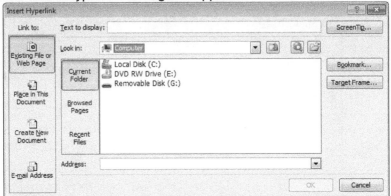

10 For **Text to Display**, type the text you want displayed for the hyperlink.

11 Select Doc2.

If you do not see Doc2 in the list, click 📂 to find and select it.

12 Click **Bookmark**.

The Select Place in Document dialog box appears.

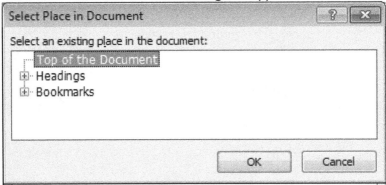

13 Select the bookmark.

14 Click **OK** to close the Select Place in Document dialog box.

15 Click **OK** to close the Insert Hyperlink dialog box.

The hyperlink appears in the document.

16 Save Doc1.

How do I insert one document into another?

You can insert a Word document into another Word document. For example, you could add another Word document to the end of your document as an appendix, or you could add a Word document into the middle of your document as a new chapter.

To insert a Word document:

1 Position the insertion point where you want to insert the document.

2 Select the **Insert** tab.
   —OR—
   Press **Alt+N**.

3 Click the arrow beside the **Object** button in the **Text** group.

4 Select **Text from File**.
   The Insert File dialog box appears.

5 Select the document you want to insert.

6 Click **OK**.

How do I insert part of a Word document?

You can use the range option to insert part of a Word document that contains a bookmark. For instructions on adding a bookmark, see "How do I create a bookmark?" on page 176.

To insert part of a Word document:

1 Position the insertion point where you want to insert the document.

2 Select the **Insert** tab.
   —OR—
   Press **Alt+N**.

3 Click the arrow beside the **Object** button in the **Text** group.

☐ Object ▾

4 Select **Text from File**.
The Insert File dialog box appears.

5 Select the document you want to insert.

6 Click **Range**.
The Enter Text dialog box appears.

Enter Text	? ✕
Range:	
Type the bookmark name or range of Microsoft Excel cells you want to insert	
	OK Cancel

7 Select the bookmark or, for Excel, the range of cells you want to insert.

8 Click **OK**.

How do I create a master document?

You can create a master document to organize a set of Word documents. For example, you could combine separate "chapter" documents into one master document.

To create a master document, you can either divide an existing document into subdocuments, or you can insert existing subdocuments into a master document.

To create a master document by dividing an existing document into subdocuments:

1 Select the **View** tab.
—OR—
Press **Alt+W**.

2 Click the **Outline** button in the **Document Views** group.

 Outline

3 Review the outline and make sure each section that should become a new document is formatted as a heading.

4 Click the **Show Document** button in the **Master Document** group.

Show
Document

5 Highlight the content that should become the subdocument.

6 Click the **Create** button in the **Master Document** group.

Create

Word inserts a section break before and after the new subdocument.

7 Repeat steps 5 and 6 to create all of the subdocuments.

8 Save the master document.
Word saves the master document and saves each subdocument with a filename based on the text of the first heading in the subdocument. For example, a subdocument that begins with an "Overview" heading will be saved as "Overview.docx."

To create a master document by inserting subdocuments into a master document:

1 Select the **View** tab.
—OR—
Press **Alt+W**.

2 Click the **Outline** button in the **Document Views** group.

3 Position the cursor where you want to insert the subdocument.

4 Click the **Show Document** button in the **Master Document** group.

Show
Document

5 Click the **Insert** button in the **Master Document** group.

 Insert

The Insert subdocument dialog box appears.

6 Select the document you want to insert and click **Open**. The document is inserted into your document.

7 Insert the other documents you want to include.

8 Save the master document.

Office integration

How do I insert an Excel spreadsheet?

You can insert an Excel spreadsheet into a Word document. For example, you might insert sales totals into a company report.

To insert an Excel spreadsheet:

1 Position the insertion point where you want to insert the spreadsheet.

2 Select the **Insert** tab.
   —OR—
   Press **Alt+N**.

3 Click the arrow beside the **Object** button in the **Text** group.

4 Select **Text from File**.
   The Insert File dialog box appears.

5 Select the spreadsheet you want to insert.

6 Click **OK**.

How do I insert part of an Excel spreadsheet?

If you don't need to insert an entire spreadsheet, you can insert a range of cells. For example, you could insert the January daily sales totals into a monthly sales report.

To insert a range of cells from an Excel spreadsheet:

1 Position the insertion point where you want to insert the range of cells.

2 Select the **Insert** tab.
—OR—
Press **Alt+N**.

3 Click the arrow beside the **Object** button in the **Text** group.

4 Select **Text from File**.
The Insert File dialog box appears.

5 Select the spreadsheet you want to insert.

6 Click **Range**.
The Enter Text dialog box appears.

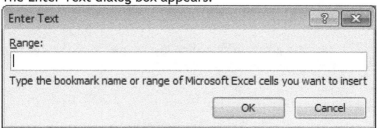

7 Select the range of cells you want to insert.

8 Click **OK**.

How do I insert an Excel chart?

You can paste an Excel chart into Word and link it to the source Excel spreadsheet. If you link the chart, Word can update the chart if it changes in Excel. If you do not want the chart to update in Word, you can insert the chart as a picture.

To link an Excel chart to its source:

1 Open the Excel spreadsheet.

2 Select the chart.

3 Press **Ctrl+C**.

The chart is copied to the clipboard.

4 Open your Word document.

5 Select the **Home** tab.

—OR—

Press **Alt+H**.

6 Click the arrow for the **Paste** button in the **Clipboard** group.

7 Select **Paste Special**.

The Paste Special dialog box appears.

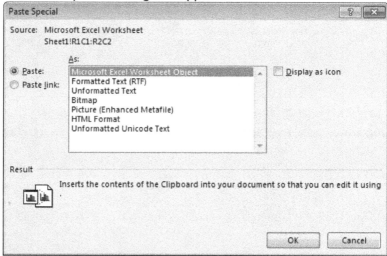

8 Select the **Paste Link** option.

9 Select **Microsoft Excel Worksheet Object**.

10 Click **OK**.

To insert an Excel chart as a picture:

1 Open the Excel spreadsheet.

2 Select the chart.

3 Press **Ctrl+C.**

The chart is copied to the clipboard.

4 Open your Word document.

5 Select the **Home** tab.

—OR—

Press **Alt+H.**

6 Click the arrow for the **Paste** button in the **Clipboard** group.

7 Select **Paste Special.**

The Paste Special dialog box appears.

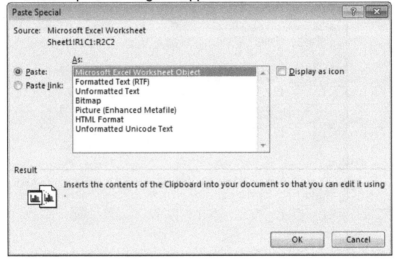

8 Select the **Paste Link** option.

9 Select **Picture.**

10 Click **OK.**

See also "How do I add a chart?" on page 255 and "How do I convert a table to a chart?" on page 354.

How do I link to an Excel spreadsheet?

You can create a link in a Word document that opens an Excel spreadsheet. You can even open the spreadsheet to a specific sheet.

To link to an Excel spreadsheet:

1 Press **Ctrl+F9**.
Field code braces appear.

2 Within the braces, type:
HYPERLINK "C:\\MyExcelFile.xls"

using your file's path and filename. Be sure to use double back slashes ("\\") in your path name.

TIP *If you want to link to a page in the spreadsheet, type:*
HYPERLINK "C:\\MyExcelFile.xls#MySheet"

If your sheet name contains a space, it must be enclosed in single quote marks: HYPERLINK "C:\\MyExcelFile.xls#'My Sheet'"

3 Press **F9**.
The field code is replaced with the hyperlink.

TIP *You can use the \o switch (lower-case "o") to add a tooltip to a hyperlink:*

{ HYPERLINK "C:\\MyExcelFile.xls" \o "Click here to open the sample Excel file" }

How do I link to a range from Excel?

You can insert part of an Excel spreadsheet into a Word document.

To insert a range from an Excel spreadsheet:

1 Press **Ctrl+F9**.
Field code braces appear.

2 Within the braces, type:
HYPERLINK "C:\\MyExcelFile.xls#'Sheet 1'!Range

using your file's path and filename, the name of the sheet, and the range. Be sure to use double back slashes ("\\") in your path name.

3 Press **F9.**
The field code is replaced with the hyperlink.

How do I update link paths?

When you create a link to another Word, PowerPoint, or Excel document or insert a picture as a reference, the link's path contains the folder name where you store the document or picture. If you have a lot of links and need to move the documents or pictures, you can the Find and Replace feature to update the link paths.

To change the links paths in a document:

1 Select the **View** tab.
—OR—
Press **Alt+W.**

2 Click the **Draft** button in the **Document Views** group.

3 Press **Alt+F9** to display the field codes.

4 Press **Ctrl+H.**
The Find and Replace dialog box appears with the Replace tab selected.

5 In the **Find** box, type the old path.

> 📖▷ *You can copy and paste the path from a link in your document to make sure it's typed correctly.*

6 In the **Replace** box, type the new path.

7 Click **Replace All.**
The paths are updated.

8 Click **Close.**

9 Press **Alt+F9** to display the field results.

10 Select the entire document by pressing **Ctrl+A.**

11 Press **F9.**
Word updates all the fields in the document.

How do I link to a PowerPoint presentation?

You can link to a PowerPoint presentation from a Word document. You can even link to a specific slide.

To link to a PowerPoint presentation:

1 Highlight the text to which you want to attach the hyperlink.

2 Press **Ctrl+K.**
The Insert Hyperlink dialog box appears.

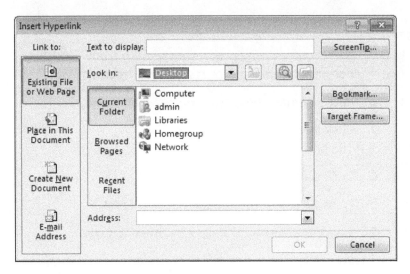

3   Select **Existing File or Web Page**.

4   In the **Look In** area, select **Current Folder**.

5   Select the PowerPoint presentation.
    The full path to the file appears at the bottom of the dialog
    box, in the Address box.

6   At the end of the address, type a pound sign (#) followed by
    the slide number you want to use from the presentation.
    For instance, if you want to use the third slide, type **#3**.

7   Click **OK**.

How do I open a link?

If you insert information from another document, you can open
the other document from Word.

To open a link to another document:

☐   Double-click the linked item.
    —OR—
    Right-click the linked item, select **Linked Object**, and select
    Open Link.

How do I update or break a link to a document?

When you link to a document, changes made in the source document also appear in your document.

If you do not want the content to be updated, you can break the link. The content will stay in your document, but changes in the source document will not appear in your document. If the source document moves, you should update the link to include the file's new location.

◇ *The Edit Links to Files button is not included by default in the ribbon, so you will need to add it to a tab. See "How do I add buttons to a ribbon group?" on page 283 for more information.*

To break a link to a document:

1   Select the tab that contains your "Edit Links to Files" button.

2   Click **Edit Links to Files**.
    The Links dialog box appears.

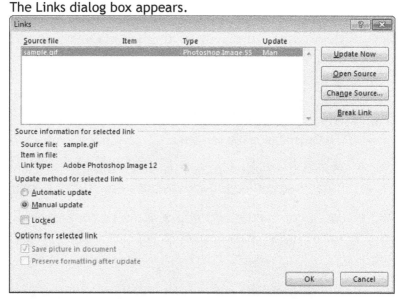

3   Select the link you want to break or update.

4 To break the link, click **Break Link** and click **OK**.
To update the link, click **Change Source**, select the file, and
click **Open**.

5 Click **OK**.

How do I create a PowerPoint presentation from a Word outline?

When you create a PowerPoint presentation from a Word
outline, any text formatted with the "Heading 1" style will
become a new slide.

To create a PowerPoint presentation from a Word outline:

1 Create and save the outline in Word.

2 Close the Word document.

3 Open PowerPoint.

4 In PowerPoint, select the **Home** tab.

5 Click the **New Slide** button and select **Slides from Outline**.

The Open dialog box appears.

6 Select the Word document and click **Open**.
The Word outline is converted to a PowerPoint presentation

◇ *If you change the PowerPoint presentation, the changes will not
appear in the original Word document.*

Opening

How do I quickly create a new blank document?

You can press **Ctrl+N** to create a new document based on the Normal template.

How do I automatically open a new document when I open Word?

By default, the Start screen appears when you open Word. You can change this setting to automatically open a new document when you open Word.

To automatically open a new document when you open Word:

1 Select **File > Options.**
   The Word Options dialog box appears.

2 Select the **General** tab.

3 Clear the **Show the Start screen when the application starts** check box.

4 Click **OK.**

How do I find a document I was working with yesterday?

Word keeps a list of your recently-opened documents. To open a document you were recently working with, select **File > Open.** Your recent documents will be listed on the left. To clear the list of recent documents, see "How do I remove my list of recent documents" on page 221.

How do I open documents faster by using draft fonts?

If you are creating a large document, it may be slow to open or scroll. You can use the Draft Fonts feature to drastically speed up a document. The Draft Fonts feature displays all text using a selected font and size. It also disables some features, such as displaying graphics, bullets, and special characters.

◊ *The Draft Fonts feature affects only the display of your document; it does not change your document.*

To use draft fonts:

1   Select **File** > **Options**.
    The Word Options dialog box appears.

2   Select the **Advanced** tab.

3   Scroll down to the **Show document content** section.

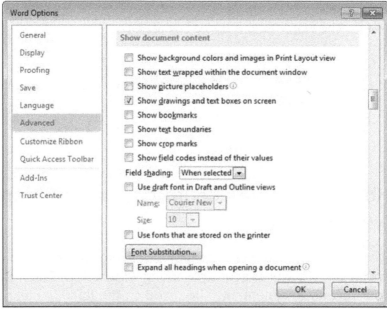

4   Select the **Use draft font in Draft and Outline views** check box.

5   Click **OK**.

How do I open old Word documents?

Word may prevent old documents from opening to protect you from viruses or other security issues. If you only open safe documents from known sources, you can allow Word to open old documents.

To open old Word documents:

1   Select **File** > **Options**.
    The Word Options dialog box appears.

2   Select the **Trust Center** tab.

3   Click **Trust Center Settings**.

4   Select the **File Block Settings** tab.

5   Select the **Open** checkbox for the document types you would like to open.

6   Select **Open selected file types in protected view**.

7   Click **OK** to close the Trust Center dialog box.

8   Click **OK** to close the Word Options dialog box.

How do I open a document in an old version of Word?

You will need to download the free Microsoft Office Compatibility Pack to open new Word documents in older versions of Word. It's available at:

http://goo.gl/45kJF

The following features will change in older versions of Word:

Feature	How it converts to older versions
Bibliography	Converted to text.
Charts and diagrams	Some charts and diagrams are converted to images and cannot be changed.
Citations	Converted to text.
Content controls	Converted to text.
Custom XML	Not supported.
Equations	Become pictures and cannot be changed.
Heading and body fonts	Converted to inline formatting.
Macros and macro signatures	Removed in Word 2000 or earlier.
Mail merge data	Removed, and you cannot connect to data sources.
Margins	Converted to absolute positioning.
Office Art	Only a small subset of options are available.
Password-protected files	Cannot be opened.
Placeholder text	Converted to text.
Relatively-positioned text boxes	Converted to absolutely-positioned text boxes.
Themes	Converted to styles.
Tracked moves	Converted to insertions and deletions.

How do I open multiple documents at the same time?

You can use the Ctrl or Shift key to select and open multiple documents at the same time.

To open multiple documents at the same time:

1 Press **Ctrl+O**.
   The Open dialog box appears.

2 Use **Shift** or **Ctrl** to select multiple documents.

3 Click **Open**.

How do I open a copy of a document?

If you want to make sure you don't accidentally change a document, you can create and open a copy of it.

To open a copy of a document:

1 Select **File** > **Open**.
   —OR—
   Press **Ctrl+O**.
   The Open dialog box appears.

2 Select the document file you want to copy.

3 Click the down-arrow on the right side of the **Open** button.
   A drop-down list appears.

4 Select **Open As Copy**.
   Word creates and opens a copy of the document with "Copy of" added to the filename.

How do I open and edit PDFs? NEW!

You can now open and edit .pdf documents in Word.

To open and edit a .pdf document:

1 Select **File** > **Open**.
   —OR—
   Press **Ctrl+O**.
   The Open dialog box appears.

2 In the **Open** section, click **Recent Documents**, **SkyDrive**, or **Computer**.

3 Click **Browse**.

4 Select your .pdf document and click **OK**.
Word will convert and open the document.

How do I open an HTML document as text?

Usually, HTML documents open in Word as they will appear in a browser. However, you may want them to open as text so you can edit the code.

To open HTML documents as text:

1 Select the **File** > **Options**.
The Word Options dialog box appears.

2 Select the **Advanced** tab.

3 Scroll down to the **General** group.

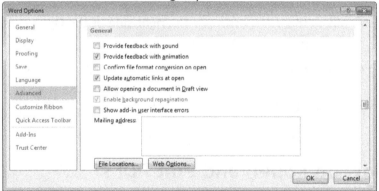

4 Select the **Confirm file format conversion on open** check box.

5 Click **OK**.

Now, whenever you open a document with an HTML (or HTM) extension, the Convert File dialog box will appear. Select Text Only, and Word will open the HTML file as text.

If you open an HTML document from the most recently-used file list or the Documents list from Windows, Word will open the document it will appear in a browser.

How do I update links when I open a document?

You can update links automatically when you open a document.

To automatically update links when opening a document:

1 Select **File** > **Options**.
The Word Options dialog box appears.

2 Select the **Advanced** tab.

3 Scroll down to the **General** section.

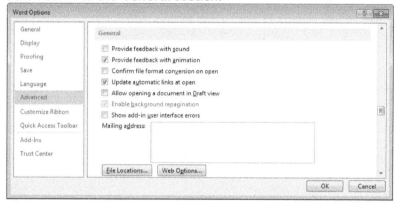

4 Select the **Update automatic links at open** check box.

5 Click **OK**.

How do I remove a recent document?

By default, Word displays a list of recently-opened documents when you select **File** > **Open**. You can click a document in the list to open it. If you no longer need to open a document or if you have deleted it, you can remove the document from the list.

To remove a recent document from the list:

1 Select **File** > **Open**.

2 Right-click a recent document.

3 To clear only the place you selected, select **Remove from list**.
To clear all of the recent documents, select **Clear Unpinned Documents**.
If you have pinned a recent document, right-click it and select **Unpin from List** first.

How do I remove the list of recent documents?

You can remove the entire list of recent documents if it's distracting.

To remove the recent documents list:

1 Select **File** > **Options**.
The Word Options dialog box appears.

2 Select the **Advanced** tab.

3 Scroll down to the **Display** section.

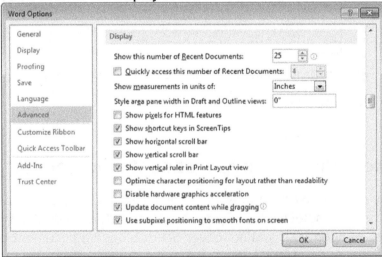

4 For **Show this number of Recent Documents**, type or select the number of files you'd like your File menu to display. To remove the list, type **0**.

5 Clear the **Quickly access this number of Recent Documents** check box.

6 Click **OK**.

Outline and Navigation pane

How do I open the Outline view?

You can use the Outline view to view and re-organize your content by heading levels.

To open the Outline view:

- Select **View** > **Outline**.
  —OR—
  Press **Alt+Ctrl+O**.

How do I open the Navigation pane?

You can use the Navigation pane to rearrange sections in a document.

To rearrange sections:

1 Select the **View** tab.
   —OR—
   Press **Alt+W**.

2 Select the **Navigation Pane** check box.
   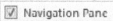

3 Click and drag a heading up or down in the Navigation Pane. The heading and its associated content will move to the new location.

How do I change a paragraph's outline level?

When you open the Outline view, the "Heading 1" through "Heading 9" styles display as outline levels 1-9. If you change a paragraph's outline level, it will also change to use the matching heading style. The "Body Text" level is used for content that does not use a heading style.

To change a paragraph's outline level:

1   Select **View** > **Outline**.
    —OR—
    Press **Alt+Ctrl+O**.
    The Outline view appears.

2   Click inside the paragraph.

3   Select a level in the outline level drop-down list.

How do I print an outline?

If you print from the Outline view, Word will only print the content that is currently visible.

To print an outline:

1   Select the **View** tab.
    —OR—
    Press **Alt+W**.

2   Click the **Outline** button in the **Document Views** group.
     Outline

3   For **Show Level**, select the lowest heading level that you want to print.

4   Select **File** > **Print** to print the document.

Pictures and videos

I can't see the entire picture...what's wrong?

If you insert a picture into a paragraph with a fixed amount of line spacing, the picture will be "cut off" if it is larger than the paragraph's line spacing setting. For example, if a paragraph's line spacing is 18pt, the picture can only be 18pt tall. A pt ("point") is only $1/72$ of an inch, so in this example the picture can only be $1/3$ inch tall.

To change the line spacing:

1 Select the picture or position the insertion point anywhere inside the paragraph that contains the picture.

2 Select the **Home** tab.
   —OR—
   Press **Alt+H**.

3 Click the ⬆☰▾ **Line and Paragraph Spacing** button in the **Paragraph** group.
   The spacing options appear.

4 Select **1.0**.
   When the line spacing is set to 1.0 ("single"), Word will use the height of the tallest element in the line as the height of the line.

How do I crop a picture?

After you insert a picture, you can crop it to only display part of the picture. Cropping a picture does not change the picture or reduce its file size. It only specifies how much of the picture is visible.

To crop a picture:

1 Select a picture.

2 Select the **Picture Tools Format** tab.

3 Click the **Crop** button in the **Size** group.

Crop marks appear at the corners and in the center of each side of the picture.

4 Drag the crop marks to change how much of the picture is visible.

5 Click anywhere outside the picture.

How do I crop a picture to a shape?

You can crop a picture to match one of Word's built-in shapes, such as a star or circle.

To crop a picture to a shape:

1 Select a picture.

2 Select the **Picture Tools Format** tab.

3 Click the arrow for the **Crop** button in the **Size** group.

4 Select **Crop to Shape**.

5 Select a shape.

How do I align pictures?

You can use the Align feature to align a picture with text or with the page borders.

To align a picture:

1   Select the picture.

2   Select the **Picture Tools Format** tab.

3   Click the arrow for the **Rotate** button in the **Arrange** group.

       Align ▾

4   Select an alignment option.

How do I position a picture?

You can position a picture as inline or floating. Most pictures are positioned inline.

An **inline** picture appears wherever you insert it and moves as you add more content.

A **floating** picture is locked in a specific location. Floating pictures are useful if you want to wrap text around a picture or position text above or below it.

To change a picture from floating to inline:

1   Select a picture.

2   Select the **Picture Tools Formatting** tab.

3   Click the **Wrap Text** button in the **Arrange** group.

Wrap
Text ▾

4   Select **In line with Text**.

To make a picture float:

1   Select a picture.

2   Select the **Picture Tools Formatting** tab.

3   Click the **Wrap Text** button in the **Arrange** group.

4   Select any of the options except **In Line with Text**.

How do I absolutely position a picture?

When you insert a picture, it is inserted where your insertion point is located. However, you may want a picture to be absolutely positioned in a specific location on the page.

To absolutely position a picture:

1   Select the picture.

2   Select the **Picture Tools Format** tab.

3   Click the **Position** button in the **Arrange** group.

4 Click **More Layout Options.**

The Layout dialog box appears.

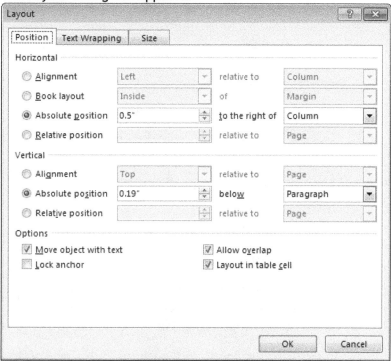

5 Select the **Text Wrapping** tab.

6 Select any option except **In Line With Text.**

7 Select the **Position** tab.

8 In the **Horizontal** section, select **Absolute Position** and set the picture's horizontal position.

9 In the **Vertical** section, select **Absolute Position** and set the picture's vertical position.

10 Click **OK.**

How do I control how text wraps around a picture?

When you wrap text around a picture, the wrap points define how closely the text wraps around the picture. By default, there is a wrap point on each corner of the picture. You can add additional wrap points to adjust how the text wraps around a picture.

To control how text wraps around a picture:

1   Select a picture.

2   Select the **Picture Tools Format** tab.

3   Click the **Wrap Text** button in the **Arrange** group.

A list of wrapping options appears.

4   Select a wrapping option.

5   Click the **Wrap Text** button and select **Edit Wrap Points**. The wrap points appear around the picture as small black boxes. Each of the wrap points is connected with a red line.

6   To move a wrap point, click and drag it to a new position. To add a new wrap point, press **Ctrl** and click the red line wherever you want to add a wrap point. To remove a wrap point, press **Ctrl** and click a wrap point.

7   When done adjusting wrap points, click anywhere outside the picture. The wrap points disappear, and your text will wrap around the picture.

How do I position a picture or shape behind text?

You can position a picture or shape behind text to create a watermark or to label parts of the picture.

To position a picture behind text:

1 Select the picture.

2 Select the **Picture Tools Format** tab.

3 Click the **Wrap Text** button in the **Arrange** group.

4 Select **Behind Text**.
   The picture is positioned behind the text.

To position a shape behind text:

1 Select the shape.

2 Select the **Format** tab.

3 Click the down arrow next to the **Send Backward** button in the **Arrange** group.

4 Select **Send Behind Text**.
   The picture moves behind the text.

How do I select a picture or shape that is behind text?

If you position a picture or shape behind text, you can use the Select Object feature to select it.

To select a picture or shape that is behind text:

1 Select the **Home** tab.
   —OR—
   Press **Alt+H**.

2 Click the **Select** button in the **Editing** group.

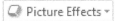

3 Select **Select Objects**.

4 Select the picture or shape.

5 When you are finished editing the picture or shape, press **Esc** to turn off the Select Objects feature.

How do I add an effect like a shadow to a picture?

You can enhance a picture by adding bevels, glows, reflections, shadows, soft edges, or 3-D rotations.

To add an effect to a picture:

1 Select a picture.
To add the same effect to multiple pictures, select the first picture, and press and hold **Ctrl** while you click other pictures.

2 Select the **Picture Tools Format** tab.

3 Click the **Picture Effects** button in the **Picture Styles** group.

Picture Effects ▾

4 Select an effect.
To select a customized effect, select **Options** at the bottom of the effect list.

To remove an effect from a picture:

1 Select the picture.

2 Select the **Picture Tools Format** tab.

3 Click the **Picture Effects** button in the **Picture Styles** group.

Picture Effects ▾

4 Select the effect you want to remove.

5 Select the option to remove the effect.
For example, if you want to remove a shadow, select **No Shadow**.

How do I apply an artistic effect to a picture?

You can apply artistic effects to a picture to make it look like a sketch, drawing, or painting. You can apply only one artistic effect at a time to a picture. If you apply a new effect, the previous effect will be removed.

Original   Chalk Sketch effect   Cement effect

✎ *A picture may look different after it is compressed. If you compress your pictures, compress them before you apply an artistic effect.*

To apply an artistic effect:

1 Select a picture.

2 Select the **Picture Tools Format** tab.

3 Click the **Artistic Effects** button in the **Adjust** group.

    🔲 Artistic Effects ▾

4 Select an effect.
When you move your mouse over an effect, a preview of the effect will appear.

5 To fine tune the artistic effect, click **Artistic Effects** button and select **Artistic Effects Options**.

To remove an artistic effect:

1   Select the picture with the artistic effect that you want to remove.

2   Select the **Format** tab.

3   Click the **Artistic Effects** button in the **Adjust** group.

4   Select **None**.

To remove all the effects that you've added to a picture (including an artistic effect), click the **Reset Picture** button in the **Adjust** group.

How do I set a picture's brightness or contrast?

If you don't have an graphics editing application such as Photoshop, you can adjust a picture's brightness or contrast in Word.

To change a picture's brightness or contrast:

1   Select a picture.

2   Select the **Picture Tools Format** tab.

3   Click the **Corrections** button in the **Adjust** group.

4   Select a **Brightness and Contrast** option.
    TIP *If you hover the pointer over an option, you can preview its effect.*

How do I change a picture's sharpness?

If you do not have a graphics editing application, you can sharpen or soften a picture's focus in Word.

To sharpen or soften a picture:

1   Select a picture.

2   Select the **Picture Tools Format** tab.

3   Click the **Corrections** button in the **Adjust** group.

4   Select a **Sharpen or Soften** option.

TIP *If you hover the pointer over an option, you can preview its effect.*

How do I change a picture's color?

You can adjust the color intensity (saturation) or color tone (temperature) of a picture, or you can recolor it.

To change a picture's color:

1   Select a picture.

2   Select the **Picture Tools Format** tab.

3   Click the **Color** button In the **Adjust** group.

4   Select a **Color Saturation**, **Color Tone**, or **Recolor** option.

How do I change the transparency color?

You can make one color in a picture transparent. For example, you could make a company logo's background transparent to use it as a watermark.

TIP *Pictures often contain thousands or millions of colors, so making one color transparent may not have much of an effect. You can use a graphics application to make more than one color transparent or to reduce the number of colors in the picture.*

To change the transparency color:

1 Select a picture.

2 Select the **Picture Tools Format** tab.

3 Click the **Color** button In the **Adjust** group.

4 Click **Set Transparent Color**.

5 Click the color in the picture that you want to make transparent.

◇ *You cannot create a transparent area in an animated GIF picture. However, you can make a color transparent in an animated-GIF editing application.*

How do I remove the background from a picture?

You can remove a background from a picture after it is inserted into a document. You can use the automatic background removal option, or you can indicate which areas you want to keep or remove.

Original picture

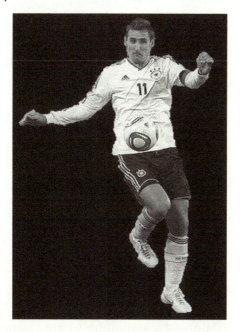

Same picture with the background removed

◇ *A picture may look different after it is compressed. If you compress your pictures, compress them before you remove their backgrounds.*

To remove the background from a picture:

1   Select a picture.

2   Select the **Picture Tools Format** tab.

3   Click the **Remove Background** button in the **Adjust** group.

4   Click one of the picture handles and drag the line so that it contains the portion of the picture that you wish to keep and excludes most of the areas you want to remove.

5   To fine-tune the include or exclude area:

   □   Click **Mark Areas to Keep** or **Mark Areas to Discard.**

   □   Click an area in the picture.

6   Click the **Keep Changes** button in the **Close** group.

◇ *To cancel the background removal, click the **Discard All Changes** button in the **Close** group.*

How do I copy a picture's formatting and apply it to another picture?

You can use the Format Painter to apply one picture's formatting to another picture.

To copy and apply formatting from one picture to another picture:

1 Select a picture.

2 Select the **Home** tab.
   —OR—
   Press **Alt+H**.

3 Click the **Format Painter** button in the **Clipboard** group.

4 Select the picture you want to format.

5 Press **Esc** when you are finished.

How do I use high resolution pictures?

There are three factors that determine a picture's resolution:

- ☐ the file format

- ☐ how the picture is inserted

- ☐ whether you are compressing images

File format

I recommend using the TIF or PNG formats. You can also use EPS files, but you will need to use the correct PostScript print driver and a PostScript printer.

How the picture is inserted

If you paste a picture into a document, Word will usually convert the picture to a BMP. The BMP format is not designed for high resolution, and BMP pictures are much larger than PNG pictures.

Instead of pasting images into Word, you should use the Picture button on the Insert tab to insert a picture into your document.

Compression

Compressing your pictures can drastically reduce your document's file size. However, it can also drastically reduce your pictures' quality.

To prevent Word from compressing pictures:

1 Select **File** > **Options**.
Select the Word Options dialog box appears.

2 Select the **Advanced** tab.

3 Scroll down to the **Picture Size and Quality** section.

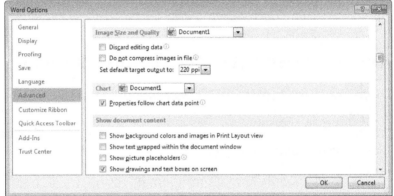

4 Uncheck the **Do not compress images in file** option.

5 Set the **Set default target output** option to a minimum resolution, such as **300**.

6 Click **OK**.

How do I insert a picture from the Web? NEW!

You can use the Online Pictures button to insert pictures from the Web, including Microsoft's clip art collection or your SkyDrive account.

To insert a picture from the Web:

1   Select the **Insert** tab.
    —OR—
    Press **Alt+N**.

2   Click the **Online Pictures** button in the **Illustrations** group.

3   Search for a picture in Office.com's clip art collection or on the Web using Bing, or select a picture from your SkyDrive account.

How do I insert a picture from my Flickr account? NEW!

If you connect Word to your Flickr account, you can insert a picture from Flickr.

To link Word to Flickr, see "How do I link to my Flickr account?" on page 310.

To insert a picture from Flickr:

1   Select the **Insert** tab.
    —OR—
    Press **Alt+N**.

2   Click the **Online Pictures** button in the **Illustrations** group.

3   Click the Flickr logo.

4 Click the picture you want to insert.
The picture is inserted into your document.

How do I create separate files for pictures in a document?

You can store your pictures in separate files rather than as pasted content inside a Word document. If your pictures are separate files, you can easily update them and reuse them in other documents.

To save a picture as a separate file:

1 Select the picture.

2 Press **Ctrl+C**.
The picture is copied to the clipboard.

3 Open your graphics editing application.
If you do not have a graphics program, Windows includes a simple graphics editing application named Paint.

4 Press **Ctrl+V**.
The picture should appear as a new graphic.

5 Save the picture.

   TIP *I recommend using the PNG or TIF format.*

If you need to save multiple pictures, you can save your document as an HTML file. Word will automatically create JPG images for each picture in the document.

To save multiple pictures as separate files:

1 Select the **File** tab.
—OR—
Press **Alt+N**.

2 Select **Save As.**
—OR—
Press **F12.**
The Save As dialog box appears.

3 Select a location for the HTML file.

4 Type a filename.

5 For **Save as type**, select **Web Page.**

6 Click **Save.**
Word will create a new folder that contains the HTML file and JPG images for each picture in the document.

How do I insert and link to a picture?

If you insert a picture and link to it as a separate file, you can update the picture outside of Word.

To insert and link to a picture:

1 Select the **Insert** tab.
—OR—
Press **Alt+N.**

2 Click the **Pictures** button in the **Illustrations** group.

The Insert Picture dialog box appears.

3 Select the picture.

4 Click the **Insert** button and select **Insert and Link.**

Where are my pictures?

If your pictures are replaced with codes, you have field codes enabled in your document. You just need to turn them off.

To turn off field codes:

☐ Press **Alt+F9**.
The field codes should be replaced by the pictures.

How do I set the default location for pictures?

By default, Word will open the Pictures Library when you insert a picture. If you store your pictures in another location, you can set it as the default location.

To set the default location for pictures:

1 Select **File** > **Options**.
The Word Options dialog box appears.

2 Select the **Advanced** tab.

3 Scroll down to the **General** section.

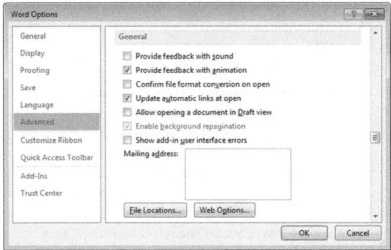

4 Click **File Locations.**

The File Locations dialog box appears.

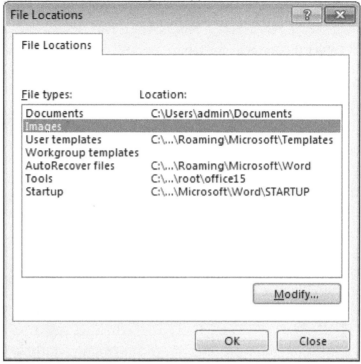

5 In the **File Types** list, select **Images.**

6 Click **Modify.**

The Modify Location dialog box appears.

7 Select a location and click **OK.**

8 Click **OK.**

How do I add a caption to a picture or figure?

You can add a caption to a picture or figure to provide a title or short description. For example, a photo of the 1974 West German soccer team could be captioned "Greatest Team of All-Time."

To add a caption to a picture or figure:

1 Position the insertion point where you want to add the caption or highlight the picture or figure.

2 Select the **References** tab.
   —OR—
   Press **Alt+S**.

3 Click **Insert Caption** in the **Captions** group.

Insert
Caption

The Caption dialog box appears.

4 Type a **Caption**.

5 In the **Label** drop-down list, select **Figure**.

6 Select a **Position** for the caption.

7 Click **OK**.
   A numbered caption appears. If you rearrange your pictures or figures, the caption numbers will adjust to the correct number when you update the fields in the document.

How do I keep captions and pictures together when printing?

You can use the "Keep with next" option to make sure captions print on the same page as the pictures they describe.

To keep captions with pictures when printing using a style (recommended):

1 Select the **Home** tab.
   —OR—
   Press **Alt+H**.

2 Click the ⬏ small arrow in the lower-right corner of the **Styles** group.
   —OR—
   Press **Shift+Ctrl+Alt+S**.
   The Styles task pane appears.

3 Hover the mouse over a style in the list of styles.

4 Click the arrow to the right of the style's name and select **Modify**.

5 Click **Format** and select **Paragraph**.
   The Paragraph dialog box appears.

6 Select the **Line and Page Breaks** tab.

7 Select the **Keep with next** check box.

8 Click **OK**.

To keep a caption with a picture using inline formatting:

1 If the picture is above the caption, select the picture. If the caption is above the picture, select the caption.

2 Select the **Home** tab.
—OR—
Press **Alt+H**.

3 Click the ⌐ small arrow in the lower-right corner of the **Paragraph** group.
The Paragraph dialog box appears.

4 Select the **Line and Page Breaks** tab.

5 Select the **Keep with next** check box.

6 Click **OK**.

How do I hide pictures when printing?

If your document contains pictures, you can print the document with or without the pictures.

To hide pictures:

1 Select **File > Options**.
The Word Options dialog box appears.

2 Select the **Advanced** tab.

3 Scroll down to the **Print** section.

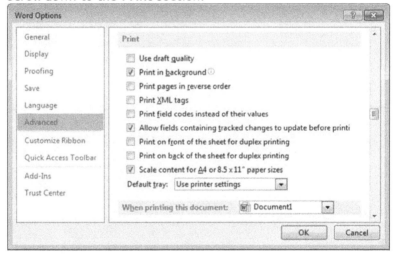

4 Select the **Use draft quality** option.

5 Click **OK**.
Word prints the document very quickly and leaves blank space where the pictures would appear.

If you only want to hide some pictures (or any type of content), you can mark them as hidden text. If you print with hidden text turned on, the hidden content will print. If you print with hidden text turned off, the hidden pictures will not print.

To hide some pictures when printing:

1 Select **File** > **Options**.
The Word Options dialog box appears.

2 Select the **Display** tab.

3 Scroll down to the **Always show these formatting marks** section.

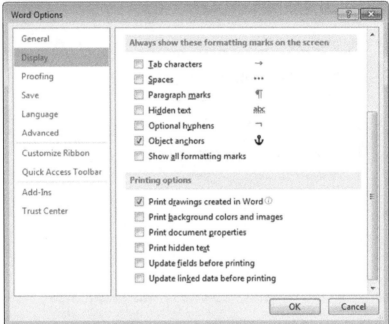

4 Select the **Hidden Text** check box.

5 In the **Printing Option** section, uncheck the **Print Hidden Text** check box.

6 Click **OK**.

7 Highlight the picture or other content that should not print.

8 Press **Ctrl+Shift+H**.
The content is marked as hidden, and a dotted underline appears under the content.

9 Print your document.

How do I flip a picture for printing?

You can flip or "mirror" a picture for printing. For example, you might mirror an image and print it on fabric transfer paper to create a t-shirt.

1 Select the picture.

2 Select the **Picture Tools Format** tab.

3 Click the arrow for the **Rotate** button in the **Arrange** group.

4 Select **Flip Vertical**.

5 Click the arrow for the **Rotate** button again.

6 Select **Flip Horizontal**.

How do I specify the default formatting for pictures?

You can specify the default wrapping style for pictures. For example, I set the default to inline with text since I use that option 90% of the time.

To specify the default picture wrapping style:

1 Select **File > Options**.
The Word Options dialog box appears.

2 Select the **Advanced** tab.

3 Scroll to the **Cut, Copy, and Paste** section.

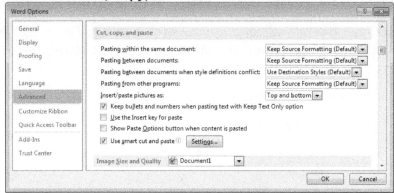

4 Set the **Insert/Paste Pictures As** drop-down list option to your desired insertion style.

5 Click **OK**.

How do I specify the default formatting for shapes?

You can specify the default formatting when you add a shape to a document.

To specify the default formatting for shapes:

1 Open a document.
If you want to set the default formatting for shapes in all documents, open your template.

2 Select a shape and set the **Fill & Line**, **Effects**, **Layout & Properties**, and **Picture** settings.

3 Right-click the shape and select **Set as Default Shape**.

✎ *The size, aspect ratio, and rotation must be set for each shape.*

How do I add a chart?

You can use the Chart feature to create line, pie, bar, scatter and other types of charts.

To create a chart:

1 Select the **Insert** tab.
—OR—
Press **Alt+N**.

2 Click the **Chart** button in the **Illustrations** group.

Chart

The Insert Chart dialog box appears.

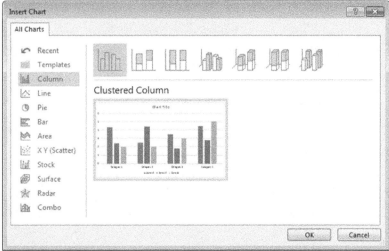

3 Select a chart type.

4 Select a chart type option using the thumbnail icons.

5 Click **OK**.

See also "How do I insert an Excel chart?" on page 205 and "How do I convert a table to a chart?" on page 354.

How do I take a screenshot?

You can use the Screenshot feature to take a screenshot of an entire application window or part of a window.

To take a screenshot of an application:

1   Position the insertion point where you want to insert the screenshot.

2   Select the **Insert** tab.
—OR—
Press **Alt+N**.

3   Click the **Screenshot** button in the **Illustrations** group.

Small thumbnail pictures of all your open windows appear.

4   Click a window's thumbnail.
A screenshot of the window is inserted into your document.

To take a screenshot of part of an application:

1   Select the **Insert** tab.
—OR—
Press **Alt+N**.

2   Click the **Screenshot** button in the **Illustrations** group.

Small thumbnail pictures of all your open windows appear.

3   Select **Screen Clipping**.
The mouse pointer changes to a crosshair.

4   Click the mouse button and draw a box around the part of the screen you want to capture.

How do I add a WordArt effect?

You can use WordArt to apply effects such as bevels, glows, and reflections to text.

To add a WordArt effect:

1   Highlight the text you want to

2   Select the **Insert** tab.
    —OR—
    Press **Alt+N.**

3   Click the **WordArt** button in the **Text** group.

4   Click a WordArt option.
    The WordArt is applied to your text.

5   To customize the WordArt, click inside the WordArt and use the buttons in the **Drawing Tools Format** tab.

How do I insert a video? NEW!

You can insert videos from your computer or from the Web.

To insert a video:

1   Select the **Insert** tab.
    —OR—
    Press **Alt+N.**

2   Click the **Online Video** button in the **Media** group.

3   Search for a video using Bing.

4   Select the video and click **Insert.**
    The video is inserted into your document.

How do I insert a video from YouTube? NEW!

You can insert videos from YouTube into a document.

To insert a video from YouTube:

1 Open a browser and find the video on YouTube.

2 Below the video, click **Share this Video**.
   A text box containing a URL appears.

3 Copy the video's URL.

4 Return to your document in Word.

5 Select the **Insert** tab.
   —OR—
   Press **Alt+N**.

6 Click the **Online Video** button in the **Media** group.

7 In the **From a Video Embed Code** text box, paste the URL.

8 Click the arrow inside the text box.
   The video is inserted into your document.

Print

How do I only print selected content?

If you don't want to print an entire document, you can select and print part of the document.

To print selected content:

1   Select the content you want to print.

2   Select **File > Print**.
    —OR—
    Press **Ctrl+P**.

3   Click **Settings** and select **Print Selection**.

4   Click **Print**.

How do I print comments and changes?

If you use track changes or comments, you can include the changes and comments when printing.

To print comments and changes:

1   Select **File > Print**.
    —OR—
    Press **Ctrl+P**.

2   Click **Settings**.

3   Select **Print Markup**.

4   Click **Print**.

How do I print hidden text?

You can use the Hidden Text feature to add draft content or information that some users shouldn't see. If hidden text is visible on the screen, it will print. If it is hidden on the screen, it will not print.

To print hidden text:

1 Select **File** > **Options**.
The Word Options dialog box appears.

2 Select the **Display** tab.

3 Scroll to the **Printing Options** section.

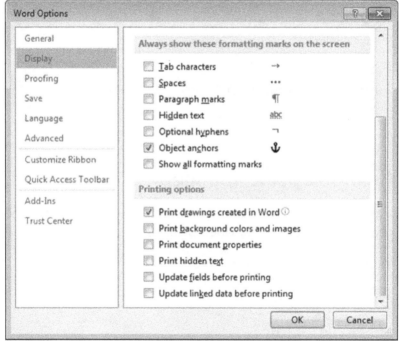

4 Select the **Print hidden text** check box.

5 Click **OK**.

How do I print the background color or picture?

By default, background colors or pictures do not print. However, you can print background colors or pictures if needed.

To print background colors or pictures:

1 Select **File > Options**.
   The Word Options dialog box appears.

2 Select the **Display** tab.

3 Scroll to the **Printing options** section.

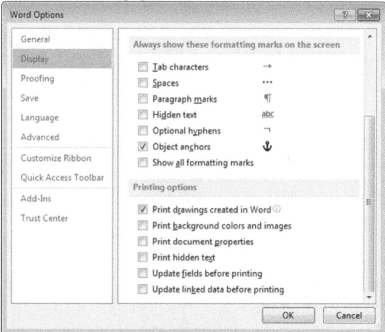

4 Select the **Print background colors and pictures** check box.

5 Click **OK**.

How do I print without highlighting?

The Highlighting feature is often use to mark draft content (I use it daily). However, sometimes you don't want the highlighting to appear when you print.

To print without highlighting:

1 Select **File > Options**.
The Word Options dialog box appears.

2 Select the **Display** tab.

3 Scroll to the **Page display options** section.

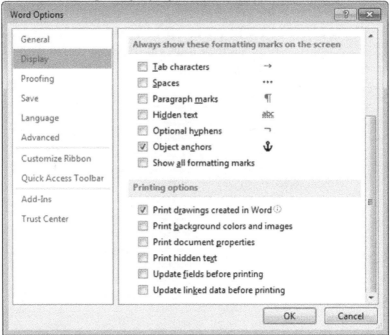

4 Clear the **Show highlighter marks** check box.

5 Click **OK**.
The highlighting disappears, but it's still applied.

6 Select **File > Print**.

7 Set the printing options, and print the document.

✎ *If you want to see the highlighting again, reopen the Word Options dialog box and select the **Show highlighter marks** check box.*

How do I keep blocks of content together when printing?

Some blocks of content should appear together on the same page when printing. For example, a heading should appear with the following paragraph, and a table caption should appear on the same page as the table. You can use the Keep with Next feature to keep these blocks of content together when printing.

To keep content together when printing:

1 Position the insertion point inside the first block of content, such as a heading.

2 Select the **Home** tab.
   —OR—
   Press **Alt+H**.

3 Click the ⌐ small arrow in the bottom-right of the **Paragraph** group.
   The Paragraph dialog box appears.

4 Select the **Line and Page Breaks** tab.

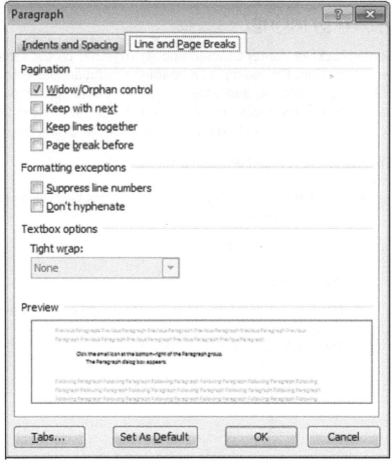

5 Select the **Keep with next** check box.

6 Click **OK**.

How do I create a watermark?

You can use the Watermark feature to print text such as "DRAFT" or "CONFIDENTIAL" behind your pages.

To create a watermark:

1 Select the **Design** tab.
—OR—
Press **Alt+D**.

2 Click the **Watermark** button in the **Page Background** group.

3 Select **Custom Watermark**.
The Printed Watermark dialog box appears.

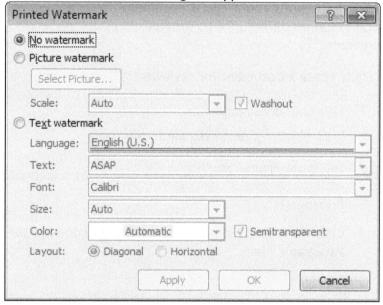

4 Select **Text watermark**.

5 For **Text**, type the text of the watermark.
For example: DRAFT

6 Select a **Font**.

7 Select a **Size**.

8 Select a **Color**.

9 Select whether the watermark should appear as **Diagonal** or **Horizontal**.

10 Uncheck the **Semitransparent** check box.
This step is optional, but it's recommended. The semitransparent setting sometimes makes the watermark print too lightly.

11 Click **OK**.

How do I triple space a document for reviewers?

Some reviewers prefer to write their review comments on paper rather than typing them into a document. You can add extra space between paragraphs to provide space for reviewer comments.

To triple space a document for reviewers:

1 Save your document.

2 Press **Ctrl+A** to select the entire document.

3 Select the **Home** tab.
—OR—
Press **Alt+H**.

4 Click the ⌐ small arrow in the lower-right corner of the **Paragraph** group.

The Paragraph dialog box appears.

5   In the **Spacing** section, set the **Line Spacing** to **Multiple** and **At** to **3**.

6   Click **OK**.

7   Print your document.

How do I collate when I print multiple copies?

If you print multiple copies of a multiple-page document, you probably want to collate the copies so that each document is printed together. If you do not collate, each copy of page one prints first, then each copy of page 2, etc.

To collate when printing multiple copies:

1   Select **File** > **Print**.
    —OR—
    Press **Ctrl+P**.

2   Specify the number of copies you wish to print.

3   Select **Collated**.

4   Click **OK**.
    The document is printed.

How do I print two pages on one page (two-up)?

You can print your document with two pages per printed page (often called "two-up") to save paper.

To print two pages on one page (two-up):

1   Select **File** > **Print**.
    —OR—
    Press **Alt+P**.

2   Select a **Printer**.

3   For **Settings**, select **2 Pages per Sheet**.

4   Click **Print**.

To print more than two pages per page:

1 Select the **Page Layout** tab.
—OR—
Press **Alt+P**.

2 Click the ⌐ small arrow in the lower-right corner of the **Page Setup** group.
The Page Setup dialog box appears.

3 Select the **Margins** tab.

4 Click the **Landscape** icon.

5 Set **Multiple Pages** to **2 Pages Per Sheet**.

6 Click **OK**.

7 Print the document.

How do I print on both sides ("duplex")?

Some printers can print on both sides of a sheet of paper (this is called "duplex" printing). If your printer can print duplex, you can set Word to print duplex and save paper.

To print on the front and back of the paper (duplex):

1 Select **File** > **Print**.
—OR—
Press **Ctrl+P**.

2 Select a **Printer**.

3 Click **Printer Properties**.

4 Select **Print on both sides to save paper**.

5 Click **OK**.

6 Click **Print**.

How do I use different page sizes in a document?

You use different page sizes (or orientations such as portrait or landscape) in a document by adding section breaks.

To use different page sizes in a document:

1 Divide your document into sections (see "How do I add page or section breaks?" on page 165).

2 Position the insertion point in the section you want to print on a different paper size.

3 Select the **Page Layout** tab.
   —OR—
   Press **Alt+P**.

4 Click the ⌐ small arrow in the lower-right corner of the **Page Setup** group.
   The Page Setup dialog box appears with the **Margins** tab selected.

5 Select the **Paper** tab.

6 Select the paper size you want to use.

7 Click **OK**.

How do I print multiple documents in a folder?

You can print multiple copies of a document, but you cannot open and print multiple documents at the same time in Word. However, you can print multiple documents using Windows.

To print multiple documents in a folder:

1 Select the folder that contains the documents you want to print.

2 Use **Ctrl** or **Shift** to select the documents.

3 Right-click one of the selected documents.

4 Select **Print**.
The document opens in Word and prints.

◇ *You can print up to 15 documents at a time.*

How do I print colors as black?

You can set Word to automatically print colors as black when printing on non-color printers.

To print colors as black:

1 Select **File** > **Options**.
The Word Options dialog box appears.

2 Select the **Advanced** tab.

3 Scroll down to the **Compatibility Options** section.

4 Select the **Print colors as black on noncolor printers** check box.

5 Click **OK**.

6 Print the document.

How do I display crop marks?

You can display crop marks to ensure your content is inside the printable area.

◇ *The crop marks will display, but they will not print. If you need to create crop marks for printing, see http://goo.gl/JHYgE*

To display crop marks:

1 Select **File** > **Options**.
The Word Options dialog box appears.

2 Select the **Advanced** tab.

3   Scroll down to the **Show document content** section.

4   Select the **Show crop marks** check box.

5   Click **OK**.

Read mode

How do I open or close Read mode?

You can use read mode to view a document without the ribbon or toolbar. In Read mode, Word's controls are hidden and the document cannot be edited.

Read mode was named "Full Screen Reading" in Word 2010.

To open read mode:

1 Select the **View** tab.
   —OR—
   Press **Alt+W**.

2 Click the **Read Mode** button in the **Views** group.

TIP *You can also click the* **Read Mode** *button in the status bar at the bottom of the screen to switch to read mode.*

To close Read mode:

□ Select **View** > **Edit Document**.
   —OR—
   Click the **Page Layout** button in the status bar at the bottom of the screen.

How do I zoom in Read mode?

You can zoom out to 10% or zoom in up to 500% in Read mode.

To zoom in Read mode:

- ☐ Use the zoom slider in the status bar at the bottom of the screen.

How do I resume reading a document? NEW!

If you are using read mode, you can resume reading where you were when you last opened the document.

To resume reading:

1 Open the document.

2 In the bottom left of the Word window, click the ▲ bookmark icon.

3 Click the screen you were previously reading.

◇ *The document must have been in Read mode when it was previously closed to resume reading.*

How do I view a list of headings?

You can view a list of headings to navigate to sections of a document.

TIP▶ *The list of headings is not specific to Read mode—it can also be open in the other views such as Print Layout view.*

To view a list of headings in read mode:

1 Select **View** > **Navigation Pane**.
The Navigation pane appears.

2 Click Headings.

3 Click a heading in the list.

Can I invert the Read mode colors to save my battery?

Yes, you can change the Read mode to a black background with white text to use less power and save your battery.

To invert the read mode screen to save your battery:

1 Select the **View** tab.
   —OR—
   Press **Alt+W**.

2 Click the **Read Mode** button in the **Document Views** group.

3 Select **Page Color** > **Inverse**.

Ribbon

How do I hide the ribbon?

You can press **Ctrl+F1** to show or hide the ribbon.

How do I create a tab?

You can add a tab to the ribbon and include your own groups and buttons. The default tabs are: File, Home, Insert, Design, Page Layout, References Mailings, Review, View, Developer, and Mathematics.

To create a tab:

1   Select **File** > **Options**.
    The Word Options dialog box appears.

2   Click **Customize Ribbon**.

3 Click **New Tab**.

How do I rename a ribbon tab?

You can rename the built-in tabs or your own custom tabs.

1 Select **File** > **Options**.
The Word Options dialog box appears.

2 Click **Customize Ribbon**.

3 In the list on the right, select the tab you want to rename.

4 Click **Rename**.
The Rename dialog box appears.

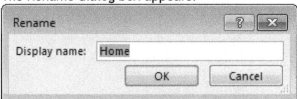

5 Type a new **Display name**.

6 Click **OK** to close the Rename dialog box.
The tab is renamed.

How do I add a group to a tab?

Groups are used to organize buttons in a tab's ribbon. For example, the Home tab's ribbon contains the Clipboard, Font, Paragraph, Styles, and Editing groups. You can add a group to a built-in tab or to your own custom tabs.

To add a group to a tab:

1 Click **File** > **Options**.
The Word Options dialog box appears.

2 Click **Customize Ribbon**.

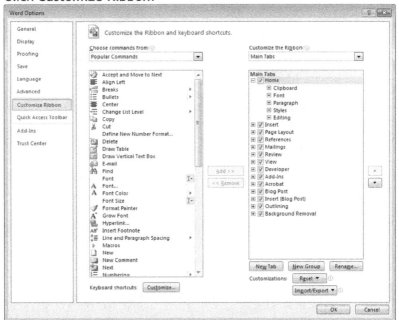

3 In the list on the right, select a tab.

4 Click **New Group**.
The new group is added to the tab.

5   Click **Rename**.
The Rename dialog box appears.

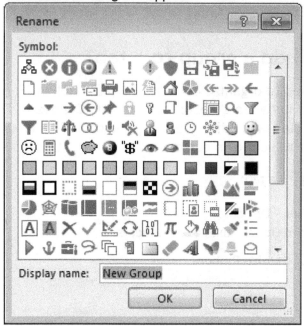

6   Type a **Display name** and click **OK**.

7   Use the arrow buttons to move the groups where you want it to appear in the tab.

8   Click **OK**.

How do I rename a ribbon group?

You can rename a built-in group or a custom group.

To name a ribbon group:

1   Click **File** > **Options**.
The Word Options dialog box appears.

2 Click **Customize Ribbon.**

3 In the list on the right, select a tab.

4 Click **Rename.**

The Rename dialog box appears.

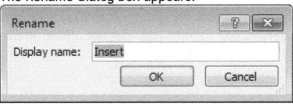

5 Type a new **Display name** for your tab.

6 Click **OK.**

7 The group is renamed.

How do I add buttons to a ribbon group?

You can add buttons to a ribbon group to organize your own frequently-used buttons or to add a button that is not included in the ribbon by default.

To add buttons to a ribbon:

1   Select **File** > **Options**.
The Word Options dialog box appears.

2   Click **Customize Ribbon**.

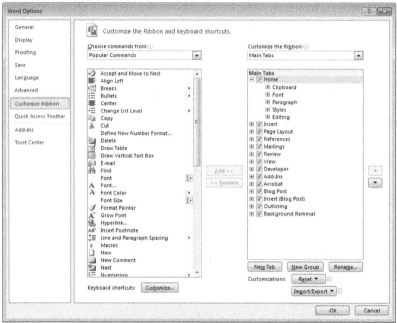

3   If the command you want to add does not appear in the list, select **All Commands** from the **Choose commands from** drop-down list.

4   Select a command.

5   In the list on the right, select a tab.

6   Click **Add**.

7   Click **OK**.

How do I reset the ribbon?

You can reset the ribbon to return to the default tabs, groups, and buttons.

To reset the ribbon:

1 Select **File** > **Options**.
  The Word Options dialog box appears.

2 Select the **Customize Ribbon** tab.

3 In the list on the right, select the ribbon you want to reset. If you want to reset all of the ribbons, select any ribbon.

4 Click **Reset**.

5 To reset one ribbon, select **Reset Only Selected Ribbon**. To reset all ribbons, select **Reset All Customizations**.

6 Click **OK**.

How do I export or share my customized ribbon?

If you customize the ribbon, you can save the ribbon and reuse it on other computers.

To export a customized ribbon:

1 Select **File** > **Options**.
  The Word Options dialog box appears.

2 Select the **Customize Ribbon** tab.

3 Click **Import/Export** and select **Export all customizations**.

4 Select a location.

5 Type a **File Name**.

6 Click **Save**.
  The customizations are saved in an "exportedUI" file.

How do I import a customized ribbon?

You can import a customized ribbon and use your preferred tabs, groups, and button arrangements.

To import a customized ribbon:

1   Select **File** > **Options**.
    The Word Options dialog box appears.

2   Select the **Customize Ribbon** tab.

3   Click **Import/Export** and select **Import all customizations**.

4   Select a exportedUI file.

5   Click **Open**.

Save

How do I set the default save location?

By default, Word opens the Documents folder when you first save a document. You can change the default file location if you prefer to store your documents in another folder.

To specify a default save location:

1 Click **File > Options.**
   The Word Options dialog box appears.

2 Select the **Advanced** tab.

3 Scroll down to the **General** section.

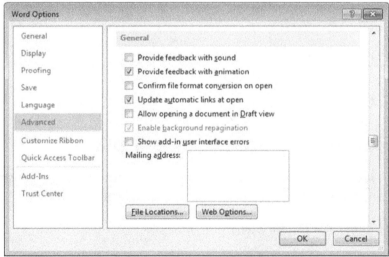

4 Click **File Locations**.

The File Locations dialog box appears.

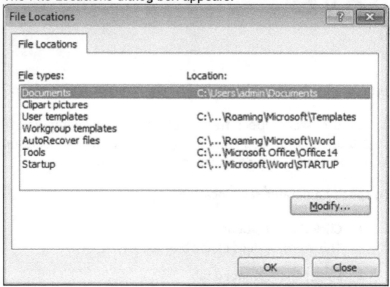

5 For **File types**, select **Documents**.

6 Click **Modify**.

7 Select a location and click **OK**.

8 Click **Close**.

How do I remove a recent place?

If you accidentally saved a document to the wrong location, you can remove the location from the list of recent places.

To remove a recent place:

1 Select **File** > **Save As**.

2 Right-click a recent place.

3 Select **Remove from list**.
If you have pinned a recent place, right-click it and select **Unpin from List** first.

How do I backup a document?

By default, Word does not make backup copies of your files. However, you can set Word to create a backup copy whenever you save your document.

To backup a document:

1 Select **File** > **Options**.
   The Word Options dialog box appears.

2 Select the **Advanced** tab.

3 Scroll down to the **Save** section.

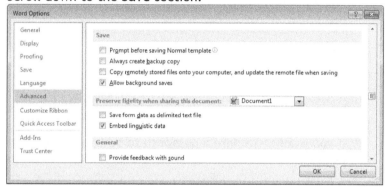

4 Select **Always create backup copy**.

5 Click **OK**.

How do I make a document read only?

If you send a document to a reviewer or reader, you can password protect it to prevent them from making changes.

To make a document read only:

1 Select the **File** tab.
   —OR—
   Press **Alt+F**.

2 Click the **Restrict Editing** button in the **Protect** group.

Restrict
Editing

The Restrict Editing pane appears.

3 In the **Editing restrictions** section, select the **Allow only this type of editing in the document** check box.

4 In the drop-down list, select **No changes (Read only)**.

5 Click **Yes, Start Enforcing Protection**.
The Start Enforcing Protection dialog box appears.

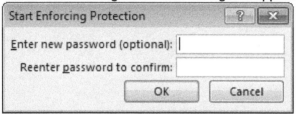

6 If you want to require a password to edit the document, type a password.

7 Click **OK**.

8 Click **Save**.

How do I reduce a document's size?

When you edit a picture, Word maintains a copy of the original picture so that you can use the Reset Picture feature to undo your changes. If your document contains numerous pictures (or if you've made numerous changes to pictures), deleting the original version of the pictures could greatly reduce your document's file size. The downside is that you will not be able to reset the pictures if you delete the original versions.

TIP *If you need to reduce the file size to email the document but still want to be able to reset your pictures, Select File > Save As to* *create a copy of your document. Then, you can delete the original pictures in the copy and email it.*

To reduce a document's size:

1   Open the document.

2   Select **File** > **Options**.
The Word Options dialog box appears.

3   Select the **Advanced** tab.

4   Scroll down to the **Image Size and Quality** section.

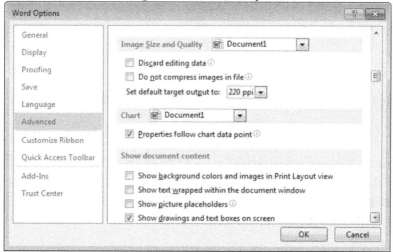

5   In the **Image Size and Quality** drop-down list, select your document or select **All New Documents**.

6   Select the **Discard editing data** check box.

7   Click **OK**.

How do I recover an unsaved document?

Word maintains a copy of unsaved documents in case Word or your computer crashes. Usually, Word will automatically open its copy of an unsaved document when you reopen Word. If not, you can open an unsaved document to recover your work.

To recover an unsaved document:

1 Click **File** > **Info**.

2 Select **Manage Versions**.

3 Select **Recover Unsaved Documents**.

4 Select the file you want to recover.

5 Click **Open**.

How do I save as an old Word 97-2003 document?

You can save a document using the older .doc format to share it with users who do not have a recent version of Word. However, any features added since Word 2003 will either be removed or will not work.

To save a document as a Word 97-2003 .doc file:

1 Select **File** > **Save As**.

2 Select a location to save the document.
The Save As dialog box appears.

3 Type a file name.

4 For **Save as type**, select **Word 97-2003 Document**.

5 Click **Save**.

How do I save as ODF 1.2? NEW!

Word 2013 can open, edit, and save ODF 1.2 documents. ODF ("Open Document Format") is an XML-based format developed by the OASIS consortium. It is supported by a wide range of applications, including the free open source Apache OpenOffice application.

To save a document as strict ODF 1.2:

1 Select **File** > **Save As**.

2 Select a location to save the document.
The Save As dialog box appears.

3 Type a file name.

4 For **Save as type**, select **OpenDocument Text (ODT)**.

5 Click **Save**.

How do I save as Strict Open XML? NEW!

Word's standard .docx format is based on Transitional Open XML. Word 2013 adds support for Strict Open XML (the file extension is still .docx). Transitional and Strict Open XML are very similar. Strict Open XML fully supports the Open XML standard, which means that documents saves as Strict Open XML should be fully compatible with other applications and "future proofed" for changes in Word or other applications.

To save a document as Strict Open XML:

1 Select **File** > **Save As**.

2 Select a location to save the document.
The Save As dialog box appears.

3 Type a file name.

4 For **Save as type**, select **Strict Open XML Format (DOCX)**.

5 Click **Save**.

Select and move to content

How do I select a word or paragraph?

You can double-click a word to select it, or you can triple-click inside a paragraph to select the entire paragraph.

How do I select non-adjacent text?

You can hold the Ctrl key while selecting to select multiple sections of text such as word or paragraphs anywhere in a document at the same time.

How do I move to the start or end of a document?

You can press **Ctrl+Home** to move to the start of a document or **Ctrl+End** to move to the end of a document.

How do I move to a line number?

You can use the Go To feature to move to a specific line in a document.

To go to a line number:

1 Press **F5** or **Ctrl+G**.

The Find and Replace dialog box appears with the Go To tab selected.

2 For **Go to What**, select **Line**.

3 Type the line number to which you want to move.

4 Click **Next** or press **Enter**.

How do I move to a section, such as a chapter?

If you use section breaks to divide a document into chapters, you can use the Go To feature to move to a specific chapter or to move forward or back a specified number of chapters.

To go to a section:

1 Press **F5** or **Ctrl+G**.

The Find and Replace dialog box appears with the Go To tab selected.

2 For **Go to what**, select **Section**.

3 For **Enter section number**, type a number or type a plus or minus sign and how many section you want to move.
For instance, you can move forward two sections by typing **+2**.

4 Click **Go To**.

5 Click **Close**.

How do I go back to where I was in a document?

You can press **Shift+Windows+M** to go back to your last location in a document.

The Windows key looks like the Windows logo: ▓▓.

Shapes, drawing objects, and diagrams

How do I add a shape?

You can use the Shape feature to add lines, rectangles, circles, triangles, arrows, flowchart symbols, stars, and callouts.

To add a shape:

1 Select the **Insert** tab.
—OR—
Press **Alt+N**.

2 Click the **Shapes** button in the **Illustrations** group.

3 Select a shape.
The insertion point changes to a crosshair.

4 Click and drag to draw the shape where you would like to add it to your document.

5 When you are finished drawing the shape, release the mouse button.

6 If you want to add text to the shape, right-click the shape and select **Add Text**.

How do I arrange stacked shapes?

If you stack shapes on top of text or other shapes, you can specify which item is on top.

To move a shape forward or backward:

1 Select the shape.

2 Select the **Format Drawing Tools** tab.

3 Click **Bring Forward** or **Send Backward** in the **Arrange** group.

To position multiple stacked shapes:

1 Select a shape.

2 Select the **Format Drawing Tools** tab.

3 Click **Selection Pane** in the **Arrange** group.

The Selection and Visibility pane appears.

4 Select a shape in the list.

5 Use the arrows, **Show All** button, and **Hide All** button to arrange the shapes.

How do I draw a line?

Drawing a line is similar to drawing a shape—you just need to specify the start and end point of the line.

To draw a line:

1 Select the **Insert** tab.
—OR—
Press **Alt+N**.

2 Click the **Shapes** button in the **Illustrations** group.

A selection of shapes appears.

3 Select a line type in the **Lines** group.

4 Position the mouse pointer where one end of the line should appear.

5 Click and drag to draw the line.

6 Release the mouse button.
The line appears.

7 To format the line:

    □ Select the line.

    □ Select the **Format Drawing Tools** tab.

    □ Use the options in the **Shape Styles** group to format the line.

How do I draw a curved line?

You can use the shapes tool to draw lines or even curved lines—if you know the trick!

To draw a curved line:

1 Select the **Insert** tab.
—OR—
Press **Alt+N**.

2 Click the **Shapes** button in the **Illustrations** group.

A collection of shapes appears.

3 Click **Curve** in the **Lines** group.

4 Position the mouse pointer where one end of the line should appear.

5 Click and drag to draw the line.

6 When you need to curve the line, click the mouse button.

7 When you are finished drawing the line, double-click.

How do I add SmartArt?

SmartArt includes graphical lists, processes, cycles, hierarchies, relationships, matrices, and pyramids. For example, you can use SmartArt to add an org chart.

To add a SmartArt graphic:

1 Position the insert point where you want the diagram to appear.

2 Select the **Insert** tab.
—OR—
Press **Alt+N**.

3 Click the **SmartArt** button in the **Illustrations** group.

The Choose a SmartArt Graphic dialog box appears.

4 Select a diagram category.

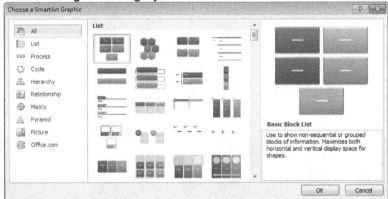

5 Click a SmartArt type.

6 Click **OK**.
The SmartArt graphic appears in your document.

How do I format SmartArt?

Word provides numerous layout and style options that can be used to customize SmartArt.

To format SmartArt:

1 Select the SmartArt graphic.

2 Select the **SmartArt Tools Design** tab.

3 Click an option in the **Layout** group.
TIP▶ *You can hover over a layout to preview how it will appear.*

4 Click an option in the **SmartArt Styles** group.

Sharing and social networking

How do I email a document from Word?

You can send a Word document as an email attachment. The attached Word document can be a .doc or .docx file, or you can create and attach a .pdf document.

To email a document:

1 Select **File** > **Save & Send**.

2 Select one of the following options:

- **Send as Attachment** to send the document as a .doc or .docx file

- **Send as PDF** to send the document as an Acrobat .pdf file

  An email message window appears that includes the filename of the current file as the message subject and the file as an attachment.

3 Send the email.

How do I link Word to my SkyDrive or Office 365 SharePoint account?

You can link Word to your SkyDrive or Office 365 SharePoint account to save documents in the cloud (i.e., the Web) and share them with other people.

To link to your SkyDrive or Office 365 SharePoint account:

1   Select **File** > **Save As.**

2   Click **Add Place.**

3   Select **SkyDrive.**

4   Type your **User Name** and **Password.**

5   Click **OK.**
     Your SkyDrive or Office 365 SharePoint account is added as a Save As "Place."

How do I save a document to the cloud?

If you link Word to your SkyDrive or Office 365 SharePoint account, you can save documents to the cloud.

To save a document to the cloud:

1   Select **File** > **Share.**

2   Click **Save to Cloud.**

3   Select **SkyDrive** or **Office 365 SharePoint.**

4   Select a location for the document.

5   Type a **File Name** and click **Save.**

How do I share a document?

If you save a document to the cloud, you can share the document with other Word users and even allow them to make changes to the document.

To share a document:

1   Save the document to the cloud.

2   In the **Invite People** section, type the email address of each person with whom you want to share the document.

3 Select whether other users **Can Edit** or **Can View** the document.

4 Type a message.

5 Select **Require user to sign in before using document** if you want to make your document more secure.

6 Click **Share**.

How do I share a document with many people?

If you want to share a document with many people, you probably don't want to type everyone's email address.

To share a document with many people:

1 In the **Invite People** section, select **Get a Link**.

2 To create a link that only allows people to view the document, click **Create Link** for the **View Link** option.

To create a link that allows people to edit the document, click **Create Link** for the **Edit Link** option.

3 Copy the link and email it to your recipients or post it to a Web page.

How do I stop sharing a document with someone?

You can stop sharing a document with someone at the end of a review or if they are no longer collaborating on the document.

To stop sharing a document with someone:

1 Select **File > Share**.

2 In the **Invite People** section, right-click the person you want to remove and click **Remove User**.

How do I link to Facebook, LinkedIn, or Twitter?

You can link to your Facebook, LinkedIn, or Twitter account to share documents.

1   Select **File** > **Account**.

2   Click **Add Service**.

3   Select **Sharing** > **Facebook**, **LinkedIn**, or **Twitter**.

4   Click **Connect**.

5   Sign in to your account.
    If you don't have an account, you will be prompted to create one.

How do I share a link to a document on Facebook, LinkedIn, or Twitter?

If you upload a document to your SkyDrive account, you can share it on Facebook, LinkedIn, or Twitter.

1   Select **File** > **Share**.

2   Click **Invite People**.

3   Select **Save to Cloud**.

4   For **Places**, select your SkyDrive account.

5   Select **Post to Social Networks**.

6   Select **Facebook**, **LinkedIn**, or **Twitter**.

7   Select whether readers can **Edit** or only **View** your document.

8   Type a message.

9   Click **Post**.

How do I publish content to a blog? NEW!

You can publish a document to numerous types of blogging software, including SharePoint and WordPress.

1 Select **File > Share.**

2 Click **Publish as Blog Post.**
A copy of the document is opened in a new window.

3 If you have not registered a blog account, click **Register Now.**
The New Blog Account dialog box appears.

4 Select a blog provider and click **Next.**

5 Type your **User Name.**

6 Type your **Password.**

7 Click **Picture Options.**

8 Select a **Picture provider**.

9 Click **OK** to close the Picture Options dialog box.

10 Click **OK.**
A dialog box appears reminding you that information you send through the Internet can be viewed by other people.

11 Click **Yes.**
A dialog box appears notifying you that Word can connect to your blog.

12 Click **OK.**

13 Type a **Post Title.**

14 Type a **Post Description.**

15 Select a **Category.**

16 Select the **Blog Post** menu.

17 Click **Publish.**

18 Select **Publish.**
The document is published to your blog.

How do I link to Flickr? NEW!

You can link to your Flickr account to insert images from your Flickr account into Word documents.

To link to your Flickr account:

1   Select **File** > **Account.**

2   Click **Add Service.**

3   Select **Images & Videos** > **Flickr.**

4   Click **Connect.**

5   Sign in to your account.
    If you don't have an account, you will be prompted to create one.

To insert an image from Flickr, see "How do I insert an image from Flickr?" on page 243.

How do I present a document through the Web? NEW!

You can present a document online using Microsoft's Office Presentation Service.

To present a document online:

1   Select **File** > **Share.**

2   In the **Share** section, select **Present Online.**

3   Sign in to your Microsoft account.

4   Select **Office Presentation Service.**

5   Click **Present Online.**

    The Present Online dialog box appears.

6   Click **Send in Email** to send a link to the document to your readers.

7 When you are ready to begin the presentation, click **Start Presentation**.

8 If you want to allow users to download the presentation, click **Enable remote viewers to download the document** during the presentation.

Sort

How do I sort text in a bulleted list?

You can use the Sort feature to alphabetically sort text in a bulleted list.

To sort a bulleted list:

1 Highlight the list.

2 Select the **Home** tab.
   —OR—
   Press **Alt+H.**

3 Click the 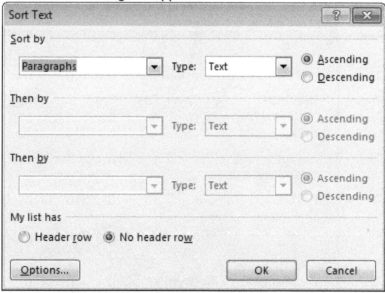 **Sort** button in the **Paragraph** group.
   The Sort Text dialog box appears.

4 For **Sort by**, select **Paragraphs.**

5 To sort from A-Z, select **Ascending.**

6 Click **OK.**

How do I sort alphabetically by headings?

You can use the Outline view to sort a document alphabetically by headings.

To sort a document alphabetically by headings:

1   Select the **View** tab.
    —OR—
    Press **Alt+W**.

2   Click the **Outline** button in the **Document Views** group.

    ▤ Outline

3   For **Show level**, select your highest heading level (usually, Heading 1).

4   Select the **Home** tab.
    —OR—
    Press **Alt+H**.

5   Click the ᴬ↓ **Sort** button in the **Paragraph** group.
    The Sort dialog box appears.

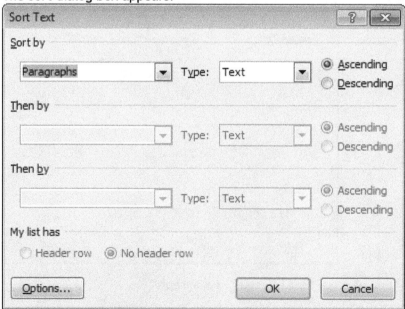

6   For **Sort by**, select **Paragraphs**.

7 To sort from A-Z, select **Ascending**.

8 Click **OK**.

Spelling and grammar

How do I spell check a document?

You can spell check a document using Word's built-in dictionaries. You can also add words to the dictionary, such as technical terms or acronyms.

To spell check a document:

1   Select the **Review** tab.
    —OR—
    Press **Alt+R**.

2   Click the **Spelling & Grammar** button in the **Proofing** group.

The Spelling pane appears, and Word will highlight the next word that is not in its dictionary.

How do I specify the language for the spellchecker?

If your document contains content in different languages, you can set the language for a specific paragraph or style. When you set the language, Word will use the specified language for the spell and grammar checkers.

To specify a language for the spell checker or grammar checker:

1 Select the paragraph for which you want to specify the language.

2 Select the **Review** tab.
   —OR—
   Press **Alt+R**.

3 Click the **Language** button in the **Language** group.

4 Select **Set Proofing Language**.
   The Language dialog box appears.

5 Select a language.

6 Click **OK**.

To specify that all paragraphs formatted with a specified style use a certain language:

1 Select the **Home** tab.
—OR—
Press **Alt+H**.

2 Click the ⌐ small arrow in the lower-right corner of the **Styles** group.
—OR—
Press **Alt+Ctrl+Shift+S**.
The Styles pane appears.

3 Hover the mouse pointer over the name of the style you want to change.
An arrow appears to the right of the style's name.

4 Click the arrow and select **Modify**.
The Modify Style dialog box appears.

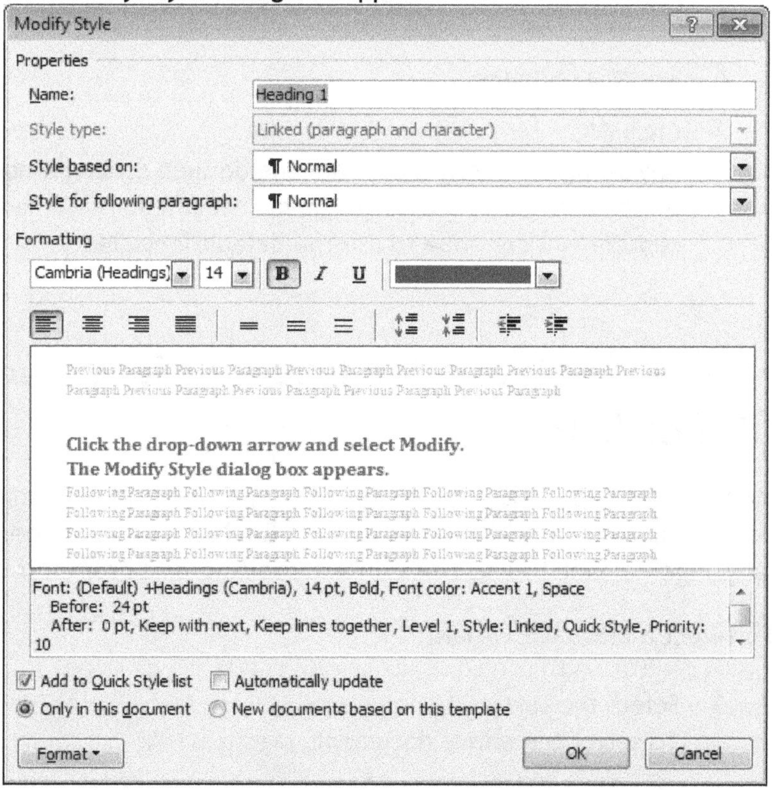

5 Click **Format** and select **Language**.
The Language dialog box appears.

6 Select a **Language**.

7 Click **OK**.
Any paragraphs formatted with the defined style will now use
the dictionary for the language you specified. The other
content will continue to use the default language.

How do I select a language variant, such as UK English?

Many languages have country-specific spelling and grammar
variations, such as UK English and US English. You can specify a
language variant to use the correct spelling and grammar rules.

To select a language variant:

1 Select the text.
To select the entire document, press **Ctrl+A**.

2 Select the **Review** tab.
—OR—
Press **Alt+R**.

3 Click the **Language** button in the **Language** group.

4 Select **Set Proofing Language**.
The Language dialog box appears.

5 Select a language.

6 Click **OK**.
Word marks spellings and grammar differences using the language you selected.

How do I turn off spellchecking for words with numb3rs?

If your document includes mathematical or scientific equations such as $E=mc^2$ or H_2O, you can turn off spellchecking for words with numbers so these equations are not marked as misspelled.

To turn off spellchecking for words with numbers:

1 Select **File** > **Options**.
The Word Options dialog box appears.

2 Select the **Proofing** tab.

3 Scroll down to the **When correcting spelling in Microsoft Office programs** section.

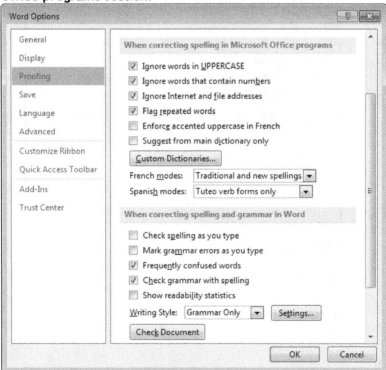

4 Uncheck the **Ignore words that contain numbers** check box.

5 Click **OK**.

How do I turn off spellchecking for URLs?

If you include URLs such as http://www.clickstart.net in your documents, you can set Word to not spell check URLs

To turn off spell checking for URLs:

1 Select **File** > **Options**.
The Word Options dialog box appears.

2 Select the **Proofing** tab.

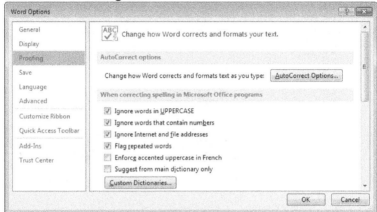

3 Select **Ignore Internet and file addresses**.

4 Click **OK**.

How do I turn off spellchecking for a style?

If you use a style for code samples, equations, proper nouns, jargon, acronyms, or other types of content that should not be spell or grammar checked, you can turn off spell or grammar checking for the style.

To turn off spell checking or grammar checking for a style:

1 Select the **Home** tab.
—OR—
Press **Alt+H**.

2 Click the ⌐ small arrow in the lower-right corner of the **Styles** group.

—OR—

Press **Alt+Ctrl+Shift+S**.

The Styles task pane appears.

3 In the style list, hover the mouse pointer over the name of the style you want to alter.

A drop-down arrow appears to the right of the style's name.

4 Click the drop-down arrow and select **Modify**.

The Modify Style dialog box appears.

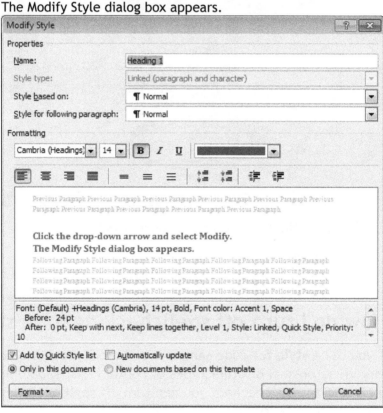

5   Click **Format** and select **Language**.
The Language dialog box appears.

6   Select **Do not check spelling or grammar**.

7   Click **OK** to close the Language dialog box.

8   Click **OK** to close the Modify Style dialog box.

How do I turn on or off spell or grammar checking?

You may have some content, such as equations, technical jargon, or quotations, that you don't want to spell or grammar check. Or, you may have some paragraphs that are not being spell or grammar checked, and you want to enable these two features.

To turn off spell or grammar checking for all documents, see "How do I turn off automatic spell checking?" on page 327.

To enable or disable spellchecking or grammar checking:

1 Select the content that you want to mark or not mark for checking.

2 Select the **Review** tab.
—OR—
Press **Alt+R**.

3 Click the **Language** button in the **Language** group.

4 Select **Set Proofing Language**.
The Language dialog box appears.

5 Select the **Do not check spelling or grammar** check box if you do not want the text to be checked. If you do want to check the selected content, clear the check box.

6 Click **OK**.

How do I turn off automatic spell or grammar checking?

Word marks misspelled words as you type with a wavy red underline and grammar issues with a wavy green underline. You can turn off spell or grammar checking and hide the underlining if you find them distracting.

To enable or disable spell checking while you type:

1 Select **File** > **Options**.
   The Word Options dialog box appears.

2 Select the **Proofing** tab.

3 Scroll down to the **When correcting spelling and grammar in Word** section.

4 Clear the **Check grammar with spelling** check box.

5 Scroll down to the **Exceptions for** section.

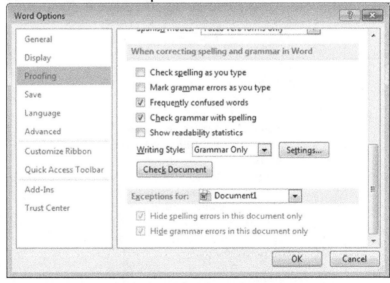

6 Select **Hide Spelling Errors in This Document Only**.

7 Click **OK**.

How do I find gender-specific terms?

Many style guides recommend using gender-neutral terms, such as firefighter instead of fireman. You can use the grammar checker to find and replace gender-specific terms.

To find gender-specific terms:

1 Select **File** > **Options**.
The Word Options dialog box appears.

2 Select the **Proofing** tab.

3 Scroll down to the **When correcting spelling and grammar in Word** section.

4 Click **Settings**.
The Grammar Settings dialog box appears.

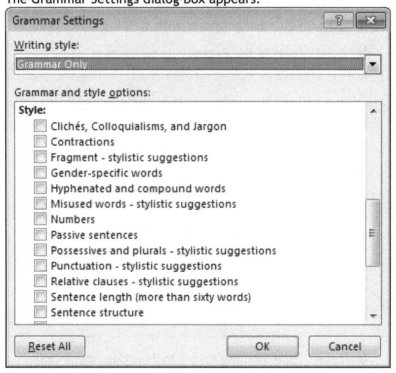

5 Scroll down to the **Style** section.

6 Select **Gender-specific Words**.

7 Click **OK** to close the Grammar Settings dialog box.

8 Click **OK** to close the Word Options dialog box.

How do I look up a word's definition? NEW!

You can use the Dictionary feature to look up a word's definition.

To look up a word's definition:

1 Select the word you want to define.

2 Select the **Review** tab.
—OR—
Press **Alt+R**.

3 Click the **Define** button in the **Proofing** group.

The Dictionaries pane appears. If you do not have a dictionary, you can select and download a dictionary from the Dictionaries pane.

How do I look up synonyms for a word?

You can use the thesaurus to find synonyms for a selected word.

To find synonyms:

1 Select the word for which you want to find synonyms.

2 Select the **Review** tab.
—OR—
Press **Alt+R**.

3 Click the **Thesaurus** button in the **Proofing** group.

The Thesaurus pane appears with a list of synonyms.

Styles and themes

What is a theme?

You can apply a theme to quickly select a design for your document, including colors, fonts, and effects.

To apply a theme:

1 Select the **Design** tab.
  —OR—
  Press **Alt+D.**

2 Click **Themes** in the **Document Formatting** group.

3 Select a theme.

What is a style set?

After you select a theme, you can select a style set to customize the font and paragraph settings in your document.

To apply a style set:

1 Select the **Design** tab.
  —OR—
  Press **Alt+D.**

2 Click a stylesheet in the **Document Formatting** group.

How do I create a style?

You should use styles to format your content. Styles allow you to maintain consistency and easily update the formatting.

To create a style:

1   Select the **Home** tab.
    —OR—
    Press **Alt+H**.

2   Click the ⌐ small arrow in the lower-right corner of the **Styles** group.
    —OR—
    Press **Shift+Ctrl+Alt+S**.
    The Styles task pane appears.

3   Click the 🔲 **New Style** button in the lower-left corner of the task pane.
    The Create New Style from Formatting dialog box appears.

4   Type a **Name** for the style.

5   Select a **Style type**.

6   For **Style based on**, select a style to serve as a "starting point" for the new style.

7   Click **Format** to change the style's formatting attributes.

8   Do one of the following:

   ☐   To only use the new style in the current document, select **Only in this document**.

   ☐   To use the style in other documents, select **New documents based on this template**.

9   Click **OK**.
    You can now use your new or modified style.

How do I create a style based on manual formatting?

If you have manually formatted text, you can create a style based on the manual formatting.

To create a style based on manual formatting:

1   Select the text that has been manually formatted.

2   Select the **Home** tab.
    —OR—
    Press **Alt+H**.

3   Click the ⌐ small arrow in the lower-right corner of the **Styles** group.
    —OR—
    Press **Shift+Ctrl+Alt+S**.
    The Styles task pane appears.

4   Click the **New Style** button in the lower-left corner of the task pane.

The Create New Style from Formatting dialog box appears.

5 Type a **Name** for the style.

6 Select a **Style type**.

7 For **Style based on**, select a style to serve as a "starting point" for the new style.

8 Click **Format** to change the style's formatting attributes.

9 Do one of the following:

☐ To only use the new style in the current document, select **Only in this document**.

☐ To use the style in other documents, select **New documents based on this template**.

10 Click **OK**.

You can now use your new style.

How do I modify a style?

You can easily modify a style if you need to change its formatting.

To modify a style:

1 Select the **Home** tab.
   —OR—
   Press **Alt+H**.

2 Click the ⌐ small arrow in the lower-right corner of the **Styles** group.
   —OR—
   Press **Shift+Ctrl+Alt+S**.
   The Styles task pane appears.

3 Hover the mouse over a styles in the list of styles.

4 Click the arrow to the right of the style's name and select **Modify**.
   The Modify Style dialog box appears.

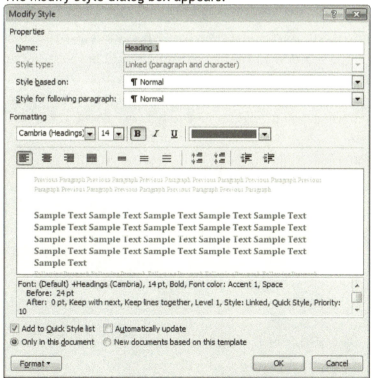

5 Click **Format** to change the style's formatting.

6 Click **OK**.

How do I rename a style?

You can rename any style in Word. When you rename a style, any text that uses the style will be updated to use the style's new name.

To rename a style:

1 Select the **Home** tab.
—OR—
Press **Alt+H**.

2 Click the ⌐ small arrow in the lower-right corner of the **Styles** group.
—OR—
Press **Shift+Ctrl+Alt+S**.
The Styles task pane appears.

3 Hover your mouse pointer over the style's name.
A drop-down arrow appears to the right of the style's name.

4 Click the drop-down arrow and select **Modify**.

The Modify Style dialog box appears.

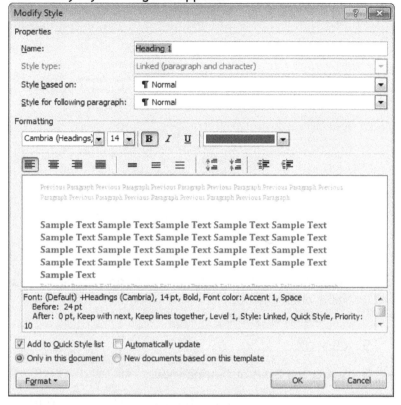

5 For **Name**, type a new name for the style.

6 Click **OK**.

How do I know which style is applied to text?

You can use the Style Inspector to see which style is being used for each paragraph in your document. This information is useful if you are editing a document or reviewing its formatting.

To open the Style Inspector:

1 Select **File** > **Options**.

The Word Options dialog box appears.

2 Select the **Advanced** tab.

3 Scroll down to the **Display** section.

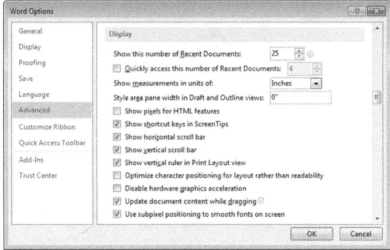

4 Set **Style area pane width in Draft and Outline views** to a value other than **0**.
For example, type.**5"**.

5 Click **OK**.

6 Select the Draft or Outline view.

◇ *The Style Inspector is only visible in the Draft and Outline views.*

How do I specify the style for the next paragraph?

When you set up a style, you can specify the style to use for the next paragraph. For example, you could set the "Heading 1" style to be followed by the "Normal" style. When you apply the Heading 1 style and press Enter at the end of the line, Word will automatically apply the Normal style to the following paragraph.

To specify the style for the next paragraph:

1 Select the **Home** tab.
—OR—
Press **Alt+H**.

2 Click the ⌐ small arrow in the lower-right corner of the **Styles** group.
—OR—
Press **Shift+Ctrl+Alt+S**.
The Styles task pane appears.

3 Hover over a style's name in the list.

4 Click the arrow to the right of the style's name and select **Modify**.
The Modify Style dialog box appears.

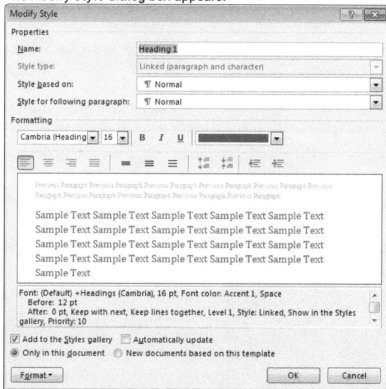

5 In **Style for following paragraph**, select the style you want to use for the next paragraph.

6 Click **OK**.

How do I assign a shortcut key to a style?

You can select shortcut keys to quickly apply a style.

To assign a shortcut key to a style:

1   Select the **Home** tab.
    —OR—
    Press **Alt+H**.

2   Click the ⌐ small arrow in the lower-right corner of the **Styles** group.
    —OR—
    Press **Shift+Ctrl+Alt+S**.
    The Styles task pane appears.

3   In the list of styles, hover the mouse pointer over the style whose shortcut key you want to change.

4   Click the arrow to the right of the style's name and select **Modify**.

The Modify Style dialog box appears.

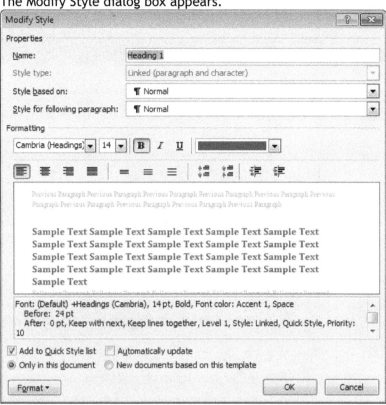

5 Click **Format** and select **Shortcut Key**.

The Customize Keyboard dialog box appears.

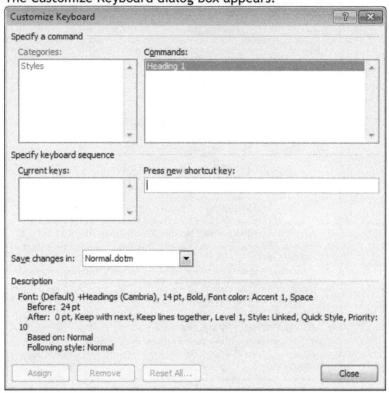

6 Click inside the **Press new shortcut key** field.

7 Press the key combination you want to use.

8 Click **Assign**.

9 Click **Close**.

10 Click **OK**.

How do I remove styles from the style list?

Word includes numerous pre-defined styles that automatically appear in the style list. If you do not plan to use these styles, you can remove them from the style list.

To only include styles that are being used in a document:

1 Select the **Home** tab.
—OR—
Press **Alt+H**.

2 Click the ⌐ small arrow in the lower-right corner of the **Style** group.
—OR—
Press Alt+Ctrl+Shift+S.
The Styles dialog box appears.

3 Click **Options** at the bottom of the Styles list.
The Style Pane Options dialog box appears.

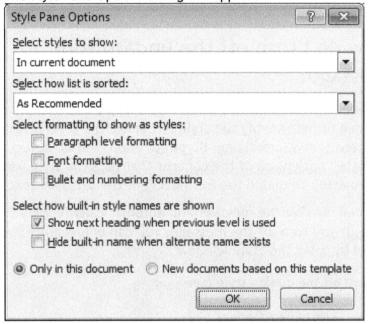

4 For **Select styles to show**, select **In current document**.

5 Click **OK**.
The Styles pane will now only list the styles that are being used in the current document.

To remove a style from the style list:

1 Select the **Home** tab.
 —OR—
 Press **Alt+H**.

2 Click the ⊾ small arrow in the lower-right corner of the **Style** group.
 The Styles dialog box appears.

3 Right-click a style in the list.

4 Select **Delete**.
 The style is removed from the list.

How do I turn off the update style message?

By default, Word displays a message if you try to reapply a style. You can either reapply the style or update the style based on the selected text's formatting. If you (or another user) select the "update" option, all of the content that uses the style will be reformatted to match the formatting of the selected text.

You can turn off the message and automatically reapply the style. If you turn off the message, you can only modify your styles by using the Style window.

To turn off the update style message:

1 Select **File** > **Options**.
 The Word Options dialog box appears.

2 Select the **Advanced** tab.

3 Scroll down to the **Editing** section.

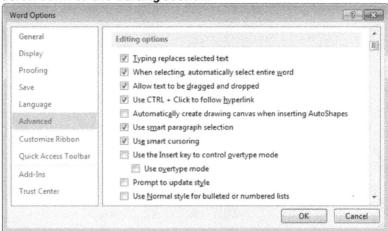

4 Clear the **Prompt to update style** check box.

5 Click **OK**.

How do I prevent users from changing styles?

You can lock a document's styles to prevent other users from using inline formatting or modifying your styles.

To prevent users from changing styles:

1 Select the **Review** tab.
—OR—
Press **Alt+R**.

The Restrict Editing pane appears.

Restrict Editing ▾ ✕

1. Formatting restrictions

☐ Limit formatting to a selection of styles

Settings...

2. Editing restrictions

☑ Allow only this type of editing in the document:

| No changes (Read only) | ▼ |

Exceptions (optional)

Select parts of the document and choose users who are allowed to freely edit them.

Groups:

☐ Everyone

🖧 More users...

3. Start enforcement

Are you ready to apply these settings? (You can turn them off later)

| Yes, Start Enforcing Protection |

2 Check the **Limit formatting to a selection of styles** check box.

3 Click **Settings.**

The Formatting Restrictions dialog box appears.

4 If you want to limit the styles that can be used in a document:

- ☐ Click the **Limit formatting to a selection of styles** check box.

- ☐ Select the styles that can be used.

- ☐ Clear the **Allow AutoFormat to override formatting restrictions** check box.

5 Select the **Block Theme or Scheme switching** check box.

6 Select the **Block Quick Style Set switching** check box.

7 Click **OK.**

What is a theme?

A theme is a set of colors, fonts, and effects that can be used to give a document a professional design. Themes have 12 color positions: four colors for text and backgrounds, six for accent colors, and two for hyperlinks. You can change a document's theme to completely change its design.

Where can I find more themes?

You can find and download more themes by visiting http://office.microsoft.com and searching for "theme."

Can I create a theme?

Yes. You can create a theme by modifying an existing theme.

To create a theme:

1　Select a theme.

2　Modify the theme's colors, fonts, and effects as desired.

3　Select the **Design** tab.
　—OR—
　Press **Alt+D.**

4　Click **Themes.**

5 Select **Save Current Theme**.
The Save Current Theme dialog box appears.

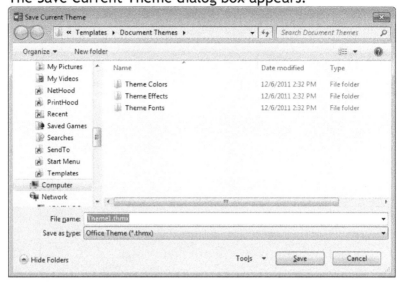

6 Type a **File Name**.

7 Click **Save**.

Tables

How do I create a table?

You can create tables to organize and format your content.

To create a table:

1 Position your cursor where you want to add the table.

2 Select the **Insert** tab.
—OR—
Press **Alt+N**.

3 Click the **Table** button in the **Tables** group.

4 Select **Insert Table**.
The Insert Table dialog box appears.

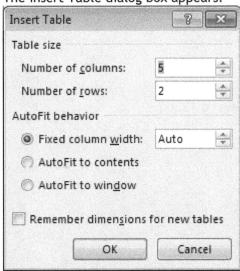

5 Select a **Number of columns**.

6 Select a **Number of rows.**

7 Select an **AutoFit behavior.**
The AutoFit behavior determines the width of the columns and the entire width of the table.

8 If you want future tables to use the same auto-fit behavior, select the **Remember dimensions for future tables** check box.

9 Click **OK.**
The table appears in your document.

How do I convert text to a table?

You can convert text that is separated by a consistent character, such as a tab or comma, to a table.

To convert text to a table:

1 Select the text you want converted into a table.

2 Select the **Insert tab.**
—OR—
Press **Alt+N.**

3 Click the **Table** button in the **Tables** group.

Table

4 Select **Convert Text to Table.**
The Convert Text to Table dialog box appears.

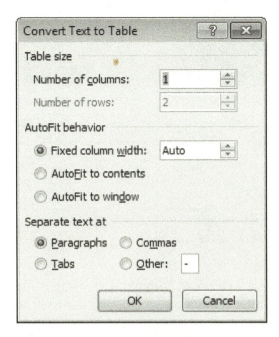

5 Review and modify the options, if needed.

6 Click **OK**.
The text is converted to a table.

How do I convert a table to text?

You can convert a table to text to remove the borders and any row or cell background colors.

To convert a table to text:

1 Click inside the table.

2 Select the **Table Tools Layout** tab.

3 Click **Convert to Text**.

The Convert Table to Text dialog box appears.

4 Select an option:

Paragraph marks — each cell becomes a paragraph

Tabs — each row becomes a paragraph, and the cell content is separated by tabs

Commas — each row becomes a paragraph, and the cell content is separated by commas

Other — each row becomes a paragraph, and the cell content is separated by the specified character

5 Click **OK**.

How do I convert a table to a chart?

If a table contains numerical data, such as sales totals, you can create a chart (for example, a pie chart) based on the data.

To convert a table to a chart:

1 Select the table you want converted to a chart.

2 Select the **Insert** tab.
   —OR—
   Press **Alt+N**.

3 Click the **Object** button in the **Text** group.

The Object dialog box appears.

4 From the list of **Object Types**, select **Microsoft Graph Chart**.

5 Click **OK**.
A graphical version of your table's data appears.

6 Format your graph as desired.

TIP *The chart will not update when you change the table. To update the data in the chart, right-click inside the chart and select **Edit**. The datasheet window will appear. If the datasheet window doesn't appear, right-click inside the table again and select **Datasheet**.*

See also "How do I insert an Excel chart?" on page 205 and "How do I add a chart?" on page 255.

How do I add a table caption?

You can add a caption to a table to describe its contents. For example, a table of temperatures might include the caption "Average monthly temperatures in the Bahamas."

To add a caption to a table:

1 Position the insertion point where you want to add the caption or highlight the table.

2 Select the **References** tab.
—OR—
Press **Alt+S**.

3 Click **Insert Caption** in the **Captions** group.

The Caption dialog box appears.

4 Type a **Caption**.

5 In the **Label** drop-down list, select **Table**.

6 Select a **Position** for the caption.

7 Click **OK**.
A numbered caption appears. If you rearrange your tables, the caption numbers will automatically adjust to the correct number.

How do I format a table?

You can format a table by applying a table style. After you apply a table style, you can customize the borders and the highlight color(s).

To format a table:

1 Click inside the table.

2 Select the **Table Tools Design** tab.

3 Select a table style in the **Table Styles** group.
The table style is applied to your table.

How do I center a table?

By default, Word automatically left-justifies text in a table. You can change a table to center or right align the text.

To center or right-align text in a table:

1 Right-click a table and select **Table Properties**.
The Table Properties dialog box appears.

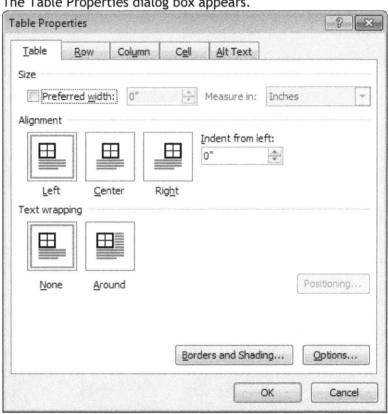

2 Select the **Table** tab.

3 For **Alignment**, click **Center** or **Right**.

4 Click **OK**.

How do I add space between cells?

You can add space between cells in a table to enhance the design or to increase readability if the text appears too close together.

To add space between cells in a table:

1 Right-click inside the table and select **Table Properties**. The Table Properties dialog box appears.

2 Click **Options**.
The Table Options dialog box appears.

| Table Options | ? | X |

Default cell margins

| Top: | 0" | | Left: | 0.08" | |
| Bottom: | 0" | | Right: | 0.08" | |

Default cell spacing

☐ Allow spacing between cells 0"

Options

☑ Automatically resize to fit contents

| OK | Cancel |

3 Select the **Allow spacing between cells** check box.

4 Type the amount of space to include between cells.

5 Click **OK** to close the Table Options dialog box.

6 Click **OK** to close the Table Properties dialog box.

How do I specify a table heading row?

If you specify the first row in a table as the table header row, it will automatically repeat if the table flows across multiple printed pages.

To specify a table header row:

1 Right-click inside the first row of your table.

2 Select **Table Properties.**
   The Table Properties dialog box appears.

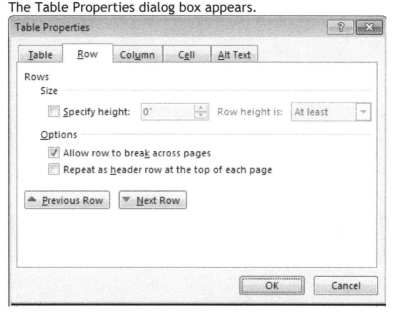

3 Select the **Row** tab.

4 Select the **Repeat as header row at the top of each page** check box.

5 Click **OK.**

How do I resize a table row?

By default, table rows automatically resize based on the amount of content inside the row. You can specify a row height to make a row taller than its content.

To resize a table row:

1 Select the row(s) that you want to resize.

2 Right-click inside the table and select **Table Properties**.

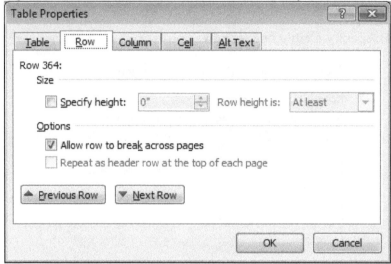

3 Select the **Row** tab.

4 Select the **Specify height** check box.

5 Type or select a row height.

6 Click **OK**.

How do I move a table row?

You can use cut (**Ctrl+X**) and paste (**Ctrl+V**) to move a table row. However, it's usually easier to use a keyboard shortcut to move a row.

To move a row up:

1 Select the row (or rows).

2 Press **Alt+Shift+Up arrow**.

To move a row down:

1 Select the row (or rows).

2 Press **Alt+Shift+Down arrow.**

How do I change the direction of text in a table?

You can set the table text direction to vertical or horizontal.

To change the text direction in a table:

1 Right-click inside cell and select **Text Direction**. The Text Direction dialog box appears.

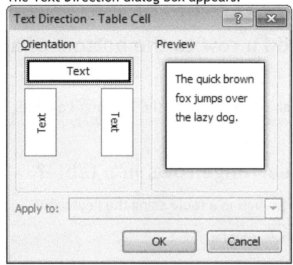

2 Select an **Orientation**.

3 Click **OK**.

How do I add table rows or columns?

You can add new rows or columns anywhere inside a table.

To add rows:

1   If you want to add multiple rows, highlight the number of rows you want to add.

2   Position the cursor to the left of the table and click the ⊕ **insert** icon.

To add columns:

1   If you want to add multiple rows, highlight the number of rows you want to add.

2   Position the cursor above the table and click the ⊕ **insert** icon.

How do I add a row to the bottom of a table?

You can press **Tab** to add a row to the bottom of a table.

How do I rearrange rows in a table?

You can rearrange rows in a table using the keyboard.

To rearrange rows in a table:

1   Click inside the row you want to move.

2   Press **Alt+Shift+Up arrow** to move the row up.
    —OR—
    Press **Alt+Shift+Down arrow** to move the row down.

How do I sort text in a table?

You can sort text alphabetically in a table.

To sort text in a table:

1 Click inside the table.

2 Select the **Home** tab.
   —OR—
   Press **Alt+H**.

3 Click the ⍗ **Sort** button in the **Paragraph** group.
   The Sort dialog box appears.

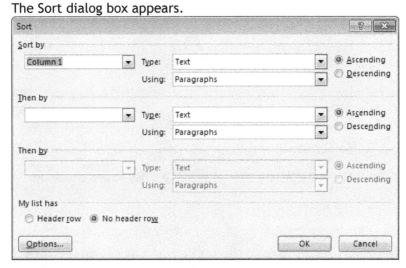

4 Click **OK**.

How do I prevent page breaks inside of table rows?

You can set your table rows to stay together, so page breaks will only occur between rows instead of inside rows.

To prevent page breaks inside table rows:

1 Highlight the rows that should not contain a page break. To highlight all of the rows in a table, click the ⊞ table selection handle icon in the top left corner of the table.

2 Right-click inside the table and select **Table Properties.**

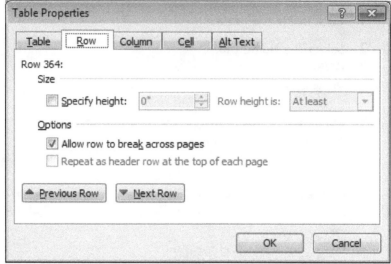

3 Select the **Row** tab.

4 Clear the **Allow row to break across pages** check box.

5 Click **OK.**

How do I delete a row, a column, or an entire table?

You can highlight a row, a column, or an entire table and press **Backspace** to delete it.

How do I delete all of the content in a row, a column, or an entire table?

You can highlight a row, a column, or an entire table and press **Delete** to delete all of the content but not delete the row, column or table.

Templates

What is a template?

Every document has a template associated with it. The template can contain styles and macros that can be used in a document. It can also help you set up a document's structure. For example, you could create a document based on a "birthday card" template that is already formatted and designed like a birthday card. All you would need to do is change the text.

How do I determine which template is being used?

You can select a different template for a document to change the styles and macros that it uses.

To determine which template is being used:

1   Select the **Developer** tab.
    —OR—
    Press **Alt+L**.

2   Click the button **Document Template** in the **Templates** group.
    The Templates and Add-ins dialog box appears.
    The field at the top of the dialog box specifies the template

that is associated with your document.

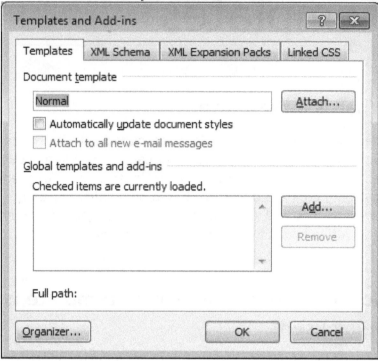

3   Click **OK**.

Where are templates stored?

By default, Word stores templates in a hard-to-find location. You can change the default templates folder to make them easier to find.

To specify where templates are stored:

1   Select **File > Options**.
     The Word Options dialog box appears.

2   Select the **Advanced** tab.

3 Scroll down to the **General** section.

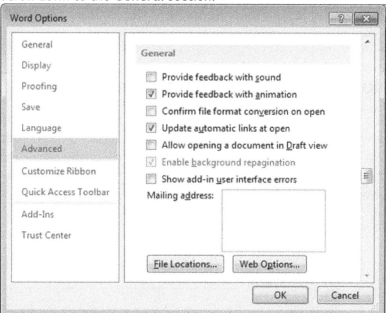

4 Click **File Locations**.

The File Locations dialog box appears.

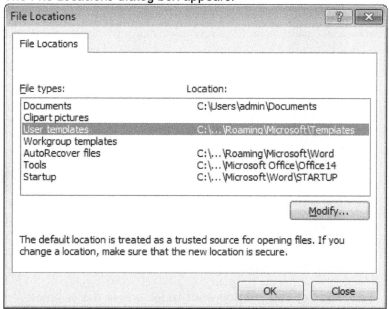

5 Select **User templates**.

6 Click **Modify**.

7 Select a location and click **OK**.

8 Click **Close**.

How do I create a template?

You can create your own templates to save time when creating new documents. Templates are created based on documents. Since the template will include everything in the document, you should start with a new, clean document when creating a template.

To save a document as a template:

1 Select **File** > **New** > **My Templates**.
The New dialog box appears.

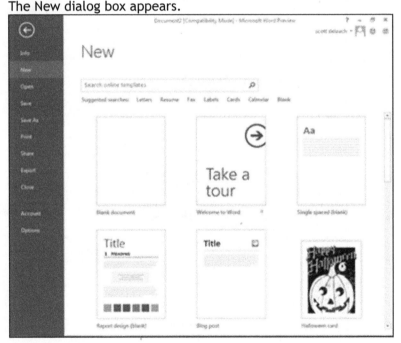

2 Click **Blank Document**.

3 Add any content you want to include in the template.

4 Select **File** > **Save As**.

5 For **Save as File Type**, select **Word Template**.

6   Click **Save.**

How do I use a template from the Web?

Word provides numerous templates, to help you create reports, calendars, cards, invitations, and other types of documents. You can also find more templates on the Web.

To save a document as a template:

1   Select **File** > **New** > **My Templates.**
The New dialog box appears.

2   Click a template in the list or use the search field to find and select a template on the Web.

How do I modify the "Normal" template?

You can open the Normal template to modify the default styles or to add or modify macros that are stored in the template.

To modify the "Normal" template:

1   Select **File** > **Open**.
The Open dialog box appears.

2   On the left side of the dialog box, select the **Templates** folder. Make a backup copy of your template (for example, Normal.dotx):

     ☐   Highlighting the template.

     ☐   Press **Ctrl+C** to copy the template.

     ☐   Press **Ctrl+V** to paste a copy of the template into the folder.

3   Select your template and click **Open**.

How do I restore the "Normal" template?

If you delete or rename the "Normal" template, Word will create a new version the next time you open Word.

To restore the Normal template:

1   Close Word.

2   Click the **Start** button in the Windows toolbar.

3   In the Search box, type:
%appdata%\Microsoft\Templates
Word will find your templates folder.

4   Click the **Templates** folder.

5   Right-click the **Normal.dotx** template and select **Delete**.

6   Open Word.

How do I modify the default page numbering format?

You can select any of the following page numbering formats:

- 1, 2, 3, …
- 1 - , - 2 - , - 3 -, …
- a, b, c, …
- A, B, C, …
- I, ii, iii, …
- I, II, III, …

To modify the default page numbering format:

1 Open your template.
For example, Normal.dotx.

2 Select the **Insert** tab.
—OR—
Press **Alt+N**.

3 Click the **Page Number** button in the **Header & Footer** group.

4 Select **Format Page Numbers.**
The Page number Format dialog box appears.

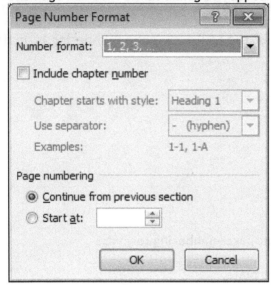

5 Set the format options.

6 Click **OK.**

7 Save and close and the template.
Any new documents you create based on the template will use the selected page numbering format.

How do I modify the default header or footer?

If you modify the header or footer in your template, each new document you create based on the template will use the modified header or footer formatting.

To modify the default header or footer:

1 Open your template.
For example, **Normal.dotx.**

2 Select the **Insert** tab.
   —OR—
   Press **Alt+N**.

3 Click the **Header** or **Footer** button in the **Header & Footer** group.

4 Select style for the header or footer.
   The header or footer appears.

5 Type and format the header or footer content.

6 Close and save Normal.dotx, and all your new documents will use the formatting you specified.

How do I "pin" a template so I can easily reuse it?

If you pin a template, it will stay in your template list and you won't need to search for it. When you want to create a new document based on the template, you can just click the template in the list.

To pin a template:

1 Select **File** > **New**.

2 Hover over the template you want to pin to the list.

3 Click the ⊷ pin icon.

Text

How do I turn off initial capitalization?

By default, the AutoCorrect feature will capitalize the first word in a sentence or table cell. Most users need to capitalize the first in a sentence, but some users don't want to capitalize the first word in tables. You can turn off first word capitalization for sentences or tables, if needed.

To turn off automatic initial capitalization:

1   **File** > **Options**.
The Word Options dialog box appears.

2   Select the **Proofing** tab.

3   Click **AutoCorrect Options**.
The AutoCorrect dialog box appears.

4   To turn off automatic capitalization in sentences, clear the **Capitalize First Letter of Sentences** option.

5   To turn off automatic capitalization in table cells, clear the **Capitalize First Letter of Table Cells** option.

6   Click **OK** to close the AutoCorrect dialog box.

7   Click **OK** to close the Word Options dialog box.

How do I change case?

You can highlight text and press **Shift+F3** to toggle between all uppercase, all lowercase, and initial capitalization.

How do I align currency amounts?

You can use a field to insert and align monetary amounts.

To insert and align currency amounts:

1   Position the insertion point where you want to add the amount.

2   Select the **Insert** tab.
    —OR—
    Press **Alt+N**.

3   Click the **QuickParts** button in the **Text** group.

4 Select **Field**.

The Field dialog box appears.

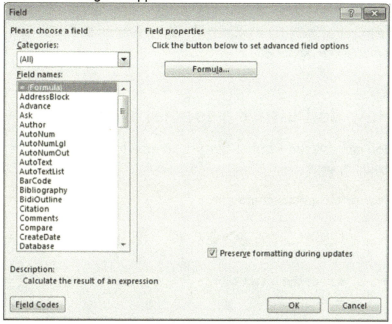

5 Select the **= (Formula)** field.

6 Click **Formula**.

The Formula dialog box appears.

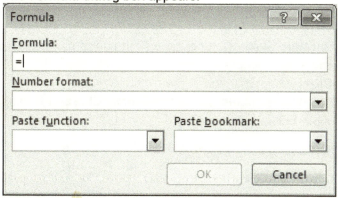

7 In the Formula field, type = and the currency amount. For example, = 11.

8 For **Number format**, select **$#,##0.00;($#,##0.00)**.

You can change the dollar sign and comma characters to insert another types of currency amount.

9 Click **OK** to close the Formula dialog box.

10 Click **OK** to close the Field dialog box.

TIP▶ *You can create a macro to insert the field. See "How do I create a macro" on page 193.*

How do I insert a special character?

You can use the Symbol feature to insert special characters such as ©, ™, or ®.

To insert a special character:

1 Position the cursor where you want to insert the special character.

2 Select the **Insert** tab.
—OR—
Press **Alt+N**.

3 Click the **Symbol** button in the **Symbols** group.

Ω Symbol ▾

4 Select a symbol.
—OR—
Click **More Symbols**, select the **Font** containing the desired symbol, and double-click the symbol.
—OR—
Click **More Symbols**, select the **Special Characters** tab, and double-click the symbol.

5 Click **Insert**.

6 Click **OK** to close the dialog box.

TIP▶ *Many symbols have shortcut keys associated with them. To determine if there is a shortcut key, select the symbol in the Symbols dialog box and note the shortcut key listed.*

How do I insert random text?

You can type =rand(p,s) or =rand.old(p,s) to add text to a document. The rand command will add content from the Word help system, and the rand.old command will add "The quick brown fox jumps over the lazy dog." You can use the p and s options to specify how many paragraphs (p) and sentences in each paragraph (s) should be added.

To insert random text:

1 Position your cursor where you want to add the text.

2 Type =rand(2,3)
   —OR—
   Type =rand.old(2,3)
   where the first number is the number of paragraphs and the second number is the number of sentences in the paragraph(s).

How do I use tabs?

You should use tabs (rather than multiple spaces) to align content. Tabs allow you to consistently indent content, to left, right, or center align content, and to align numbers or currency values by their decimal.

To add a tab:

- Press **Ctrl+Tab** to insert the current tab that appears in the ruler:

⌞	left-aligning tab
⊥	center-aligning tab
⌟	right-aligning tab
⊥	decimal-aligning tab
⏐	inserts a vertical bar (not a tab)
▽	first-line indent marker

△ hanging indent marker (all lines after the first line)

By default, Word will indent a paragraph by moving the first-line and hanging indent markers when you press Tab.

To prevent Word from indenting when you press Tab:

1 Select **File** > **Options**.
The Word Options dialog box appears.

2 Select the **Proofing** tab.

3 Click **AutoCorrect Options**.
The AutoCorrect dialog box appears.

4 Select the **AutoFormat As You Type** tab.

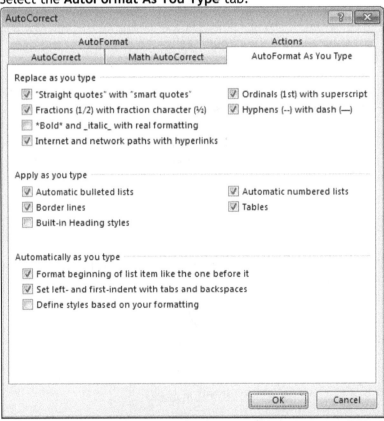

5 Clear the **Set left- and first-indent with tabs and backspaces** check box.

6 Click **OK** to close the AutoCorrect dialog box.

7 Click **OK** to close the Word Options dialog box.

How do I create a dictionary?

You can create a custom dictionary for words you use frequently, such as medical terms, technical terms, or surnames.

To create a new custom dictionary:

1 Select **File** > **Options**.
The Word Options dialog box appears.

2 Select the **Proofing** tab.

3 Click **Custom Dictionaries**.

4 Click **New**.

5 Type a name for the custom dictionary.

6 Click **Save**.

7 Click **Edit Word List** to add words to the new custom dictionary.

If you do not want to use a custom dictionary when spell checking a document, you can clear the dictionary's check box in the Custom Dictionaries dialog box.

How do I auto-translate text? NEW!

You can use the Translate feature to translate words or short passages of text into another language or from another language into English. To translate longer documents, you can use Web-based translation services.

The Mini Translator feature can instantly translate words and short phrases into 22 languages.

To translate a document:

1   Highlight the text to be translated.

2   Select the **Review** tab.
    —OR—
    Press **Alt+R**.

3   Click the **Translate** button in the **Language** tab.

4   Select **Translate Document**.
    The Translate Whole Document dialog box appears.

5   Click **Send**.
    The translated text appears in a browser window. If you hover over a sentence, the original text appears in a popup window.

To translate selected text:

1   Highlight the text to be translated.

2   Select the **Review** tab.
    —OR—
    Press **Alt+R**.

3 Click the **Translate** button in the **Language** tab.

4 Select **Translate Selected Text**.
The Research pane opens with the translated text.

To translate selected text with the Mini Translator:

1 Highlight the text to be translated.

2 Select the **Review** tab.
—OR—
Press **Alt+R**.

3 Click the **Translate** button in the **Language** tab.

4 Select **Mini Translator**.

5 Hover the mouse pointer over a word.
A popup window appears.

6 Hover over the popup window to view the translation.

To turn off the mini translator, select **Translate** > **Mini Translator**.

To select the translation language:

1 Select the **Review** tab.
—OR—
Press **Alt+R**.

2 Click the **Translate** button in the **Language** tab.

Translate

3 Select **Choose Translation Language**.
The Translation Language Options dialog box appears.

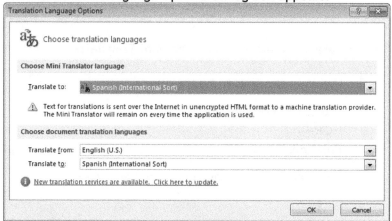

4 Select a language for the mini translator.

5 Select a language for translating selected text or the entire document.

6 Click **OK**.

How do I insert an equation?

You can use the Equation feature to add mathematical and scientific equations to your documents.

To create an equation:

1 Select the **Insert** tab.
—OR—
Press **Alt+N**.

2 Click the arrow beside the **Equation** button in the Symbols group.

π Equation ▾

3 Select an equation in the list. If your equation is not in the list, select **More Equations from Office.com** or **Inset New Equation**.

The equation appears in the document.

4 To edit the equation, click inside the equation box.

TOCs and TOAs

How do I create a table of contents (TOC)?

You can create a TOC based on the content that uses the Heading 1-9 styles in your document. Word provides numerous built-in TOC styles you can use. You can also download additional styles from the Web or design your own.

To create a TOC:

1 Select the **References** tab.
   —OR—
   Press **Alt+S**.

2 Click the **Table of Contents** button in the **Table of Contents** group.

3 Select a format or select to enter the titles of the sections manually.

How do I include a specific style in a TOC?

Usually, you create a TOC based on the content that is formatting using the Heading 1-9 styles. However, you can include any style in a TOC. For example, you could include an "AppendixHeading" style.

To include a style in a TOC:

1 Position the insertion point where you want to add the table of contents.

2 Select the **References** tab.

—OR—

Press **Alt+S**.

3 Click the **Table of Contents** button in the **Table of Contents** group.

4 Select **Insert Table of Contents**.

The Table of Contents dialog box appears.

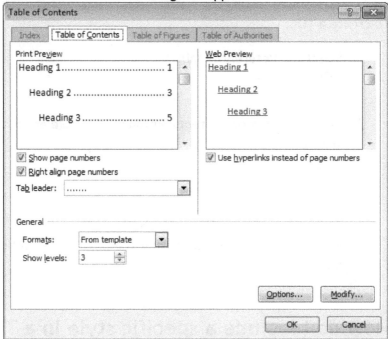

5 Click **Options.**

The Table of Contents Options dialog box appears.

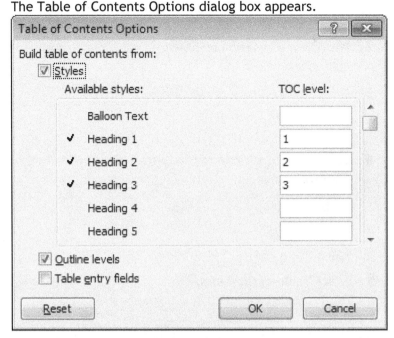

6 Type the **TOC Level** numbers for the styles you want to include in the TOC.

For example, **Heading 1** would probably be set to TOC level **1**.

7 Click **OK** to close the Table of Contents Options dialog box.

8 Click **OK** to close the Table of Contents dialog box and generate the table of contents.

How do I create multiple tables of contents?

Word allows you to include multiple tables of contents (TOCs) in a document. For example, you can have a TOC for each chapter of a book.

You will need to use unique styles for each TOC to specify which entries should be included. For example, you might use a style named "Chapter1Heading1" for the first chapter and "Chapter2Heading1" for the second chapter.

To create multiple TOCs:

1 Create and apply your TOC-specific heading styles.

2 Position the insertion point where you want to add a table of contents.

3 Select the **References** tab.
—OR—
Press **Alt+S**.

4 Click the **Insert Table of Contents** button in the **Table of Contents** group.

5 Select **Table of Contents**.
The Table of Contents dialog box appears.

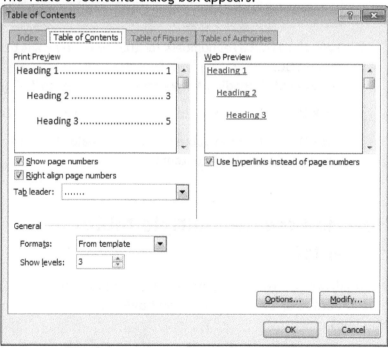

6 Click **Options.**

The Table of Contents Options dialog box appears.

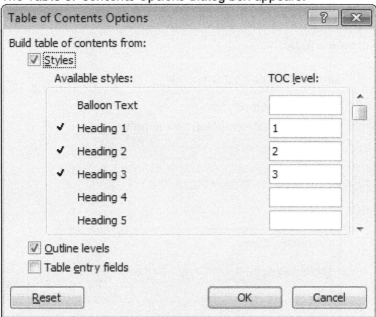

7 Type the **TOC Level** numbers for the styles you want to include in the TOC.

For example, **Heading 1** would probably be TOC level **1.**

8 Click **OK** to close the Table of Contents Options dialog box.

9 Click **OK** to close the Table of Contents dialog box and generate the table of contents.

10 If you already have a TOC in your document, the existing TOC is highlighted and you are asked if you want to replace it with the new TOC. Click **No.**

How do I create a table of authority?

In long legal documents, a table of authorities (TOA) is used to cite references to statutes, cases, and other sources for information referenced in the document. You can create a TOA by first marking citations in your document and then compiling the citations into the TOA. When you mark a citation, you can specify both long and short versions of citation. For instance, a long citation might be "Smith v. Morrissey, 21 Adj. 4d 59 (1959)" and the short version could be "Smith v. Morrissey" or even "Smith (1959)."

To create a TOA:

1 Select the full citation.

2 Press **Shift+Alt+I**.
The Mark Citation dialog box appears.

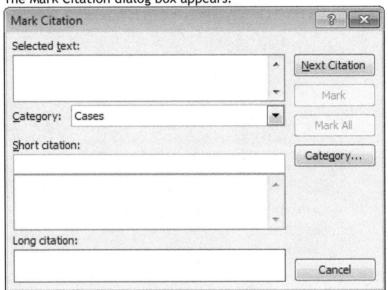

3 Select a **Category**.

4 In the **Short citation** box, type the short version of the citation.

5 Click **Mark** to mark the selected citation or click **Mark All** to mark all citations.

6 Click **Close**.

How do I add chapter numbers?

You can use the Multilevel List feature to automatically add chapter numbers to headings. For example, you can automatically number each "Heading 1" in a document.

To add chapter numbers:

1 Format your chapter headings using styles.
For example, "Heading 1," and "Heading 2."

2 Position the insertion point inside the first heading of the level you want to number, such as the first "Heading 1."

3 Select the **Home** tab.
—OR—
Press **Alt+H**.

4 Click the [icon] **Multilevel List** button in the **Paragraph** group. The available lists types appear.

5 Select **Define New Multilevel List**.
The Define New Multilevel List dialog box appears.

6 Click **More**.

7 For **Start at**, type **1**.

8 Click **Font**.

The Font dialog box appears.

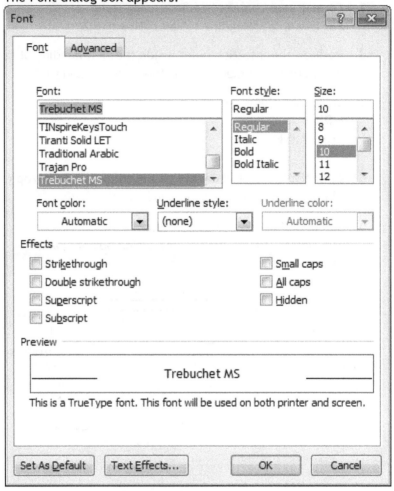

9 If you do not want the chapter number to appear in the heading, select the **Hidden** check box.

TIP *Some Word users make the heading number invisible so they can use it in the TOC, index, and with a page number in a header or footer without it appearing in the heading's text.*

10 Click **OK**.

11 In the **Customize Outline Numbered List** dialog box, set the **Number Alignment** to **Left** and **Aligned At** to **0**.

12 Click **More**.

An expanded Customize Outline Numbered List dialog box appears.

13 Set the **Link Level to Style** drop-down list to **Heading 1**.

14 Set the **Follow Number With** drop-down list to **blank** (nothing in the box).

15 Click **OK**.

To include the chapter numbers with your page numbers in a header or footer:

1 Select the **Insert** tab.
—OR—
Press **Alt+N**.

2 Click the **Page Number** button in the **Header & Footer** group.

3 Select **Format Page Number**.
The Page Number Format dialog box appears.

4 Select **Include Chapter Number**.

5 Click **OK**.

How do I include a TOC without changing my page numbers?

When you insert a table of contents (TOC), the TOC page or pages are numbered just like other pages in your document. If you want the first page of your document after the TOC to begin on page 1, you can insert a section break.

To include a TOC that does not change your page numbers:

1 Create your TOC.

2 Position your cursor where you want the numbering to begin.

3 Select the **Page Layout** tab.
—OR—
Press **Alt+P**.

4 Click the **Breaks** button in the **Page Setup** group.

5 Select **Next Page**.
Word inserts a section break.

6 Select the **Insert** tab.
—OR—
Press **Alt+N**.

7 Click the **Page Number** button in the **Header & Footer** group.

8 Select **Format Page Number**.
The Page Number Format dialog box appears.
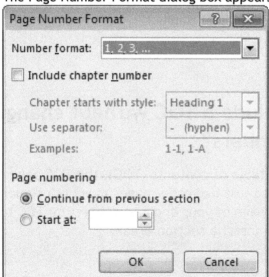

9 In the **Page Numbering** section, set the **Page numbering Start at** option to 1.

10 Click **OK**.

Track changes and reviews

How do I add a comment?

You can add comments for reviews or to include notes as you are writing a document. Comments appear in their own area of the document, and are not usually printed when you print.

To add a comment:

1 Position the insertion point where you want to add the comment.

2 Select the **Review** tab.
—OR—
Press **Alt+R**.

3 Click the **New Comment** button in the **Comments** group.
—OR—
Press **Alt+Ctrl+M**.
Word places a comment in the margin.

4 Type your comment.

5 When you are finished typing your comment, click anywhere in the document.

To find a comment:

1 Select the **Review** tab.
—OR—
Press **Alt+R**.

2 Click the **Next** or **Previous** button to move to a comment.

How do I change the comment color?

You can change the comment color and the colors used for inserted, deleted, and revised content if you do not like the default colors.

To change the comment color:

1 Select the **Review** tab.
—OR—
Press **Alt+R**.

2 Click the ⌐ small arrow in the lower-right corner of the **Tracking** group.
The Track Changes Options dialog box appears.

3 Click **Advanced Options**.

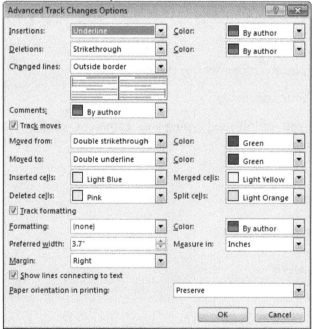

4 Select a color for the **Comments** option and click **OK**.

5 Click **OK**.

How do I reply to a comment? NEW!

If you send a document for review, you can reply to the review comments, or reviewers can reply to other reviewer's comments.

To reply to a comment:

1 Click the 💬 comment icon.

2 Click the ↩ reply icon.

3 Type your reply.

How do I move to a comment?

You can use the Go To feature to move to a specific comment in your document.

To move to a comment:

1 Press **F5** or **Ctrl+G**.
The Find and Replace dialog box appears with the Go To tab selected.

2 For **Go to what**, select **Comment**.

3 For **Enter reviewer's name** box, type or select the reviewer's name.

4 Click **Go To**.

5 If there are no comments in the document, you will move to the beginning of the document.

> **TIP** *In the Enter Reviewer's Name text box, type a plus or minus sign followed by the number of comments you want to move. For example, you could type +2 to move forward two comments.*

How do I delete a comment?

If you no longer need a comment, you can delete it. For example, a reviewer may add a comment about a misspelled word. After you correct the misspelling, you could delete the comment.

To delete a comment:

☐ Right-click the comment and select **Delete comment**.

To delete all comments:

1 Select the **Review** tab.
—OR—
Press **Alt+R**.

2 Click the **Delete** button in the **Comments** group.

A drop-down list of options appears.

3 Select **Delete All Comments in Document**.

How do I paste a comment into a document?

A reviewer may add a comment to rewrite a paragraph. If you agree with the revision, you can copy the text from the comment and paste it into your document.

To paste a comment into a document:

1 Select the Review tab.
  —OR—
  Press **Alt+R**.

2 Click the **Show Comments** button in the **Comments** group.

3 Select the text in the comment that you want to paste into your main document. Do not select the comment mark at the beginning of the comment or the paragraph mark at the end.

4 Press **Ctrl+X** to cut the text or **Ctrl+C** to copy the text to the clipboard.

5 Position the insertion point where you want to insert the comment's text.

6 Press **Ctrl+V** to paste the text into the document.

How do I paste with track changes?

If you use track changes to mark additions, deletions, and changes in a document, you may want to include the tracked changes when you paste the content into a new document.

To copy and paste tracked changes:

1 Open the source document.

2 Select the content you want to copy.

3   Make sure track changes is turned off in the source document (**Review** > **Track Changes**).
    If you do not turn off track changes, Word will assume you want to copy the text with the changes accepted.

4   Press **Ctrl+C** to copy the content or **Ctrl+X** to cut the content.

5   Open the target document.

6   Turn off track changes (**Review** > **Track Changes**).

7   Position the insertion point where you want to insert the text.

8   Press **Ctrl+V** to paste.

Another option is to use the spike. The spike is similar to the clipboard, except you can add multiple blocks of content to the spike.

To copy and paste tracked changes using the spike:

1   Select the text you want to copy.

2   Press **Ctrl+F3**.
    The text is cut from the document and placed on the spike. If you wanted to copy the text, press **Ctrl+Z** to undo the cut. The selected text remains on the spike.

3   In the target document, make sure track changes is turned off.

4   Position the insertion point where you want to insert the text.

5   Press **Shift+Ctrl+F3** to insert the spike's text into your document and clear the spike.

How do I prevent reviewers from changing content?

You can prevent reviewers from changing your content by only allowing them to add comments.

To limit changes to comments:

1 Select the **Review** tab.
—OR—
Press **Alt+R**.

2 Click the **Restrict Editing** button in the **Protect** group.

The Restrict Formatting and Editing pane appears.

3 In the **Editing Restrictions** section, select **Allow only this type of editing in the document.**

4 Select **Comments** in the drop-down list.

5 Click **Yes, Start Enforcing Protection**.
The Start Enforcing Protection dialog box appears.

6 Type a password (twice) in the dialog box.

7 Click **OK**.

How do I accept all formatting changes?

You can accept all of the formatting changes in a document and keep the additions, deletions, and modifications as tracked changes.

To accept all formatting changes:

1 Select the **Review** tab.
—OR—
Press **Alt+R**.

2 Click the **Show Markup** button in the **Tracking** group.

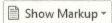

3 Select the **Formatting** option.

4 Uncheck the other options.

5 Click the arrow for the **Accept** button in the **Changes** group.

6 Select **Accept All Changes Shown**.
If you select **Accept All Changes in Document**, all of the changes in the document are accepted whether they are shown or not.

How do I stop tracking formatting changes?

The Track Changes feature is useful for reviewing the changes you've made in a document, but you may not be interested in tracking formatting changes. You can hide formatting changes and only track content changes, if needed.

To stop tracking formatting changes:

1 Select the **Review** tab.
—OR—
Press **Alt+R**.

2 Click the arrow under the **Track Changes** button in the **Tracking** group.

3 Select **Change Tracking Options.**

The Track Changes Options dialog box appears.

Track Changes Options			? ✕
Markup			
Insertions:	Underline ▼	Color:	■ By author ▼
Deletions:	Strikethrough ▼	Color:	■ By author ▼
Changed lines:	Outside border ▼	Color:	■ Auto ▼
Comments:	■ By author ▼		
Moves			
☑ Track moves			
Moved from:	Double strikethrough ▼	Color:	■ Green ▼
Moved to:	Double underline ▼	Color:	■ Green ▼
Table cell highlighting			
Inserted cells:	☐ Light Blue ▼	Merged cells:	☐ Light Yellow ▼
Deleted cells:	☐ Pink ▼	Split cells:	☐ Light Orange ▼
Formatting			
☑ Track formatting			
Formatting:	(none) ▼	Color:	■ By author ▼
Balloons			
Use Balloons (Print and Web Layout):		Only for comments/formatting ▼	
Preferred width:	3" ⬍	Measure in:	Inches ▼
Margin:	Right ▼		
☑ Show lines connecting to text			
Paper orientation in printing:		Preserve ▼	
		OK	Cancel

4 Uncheck the **Track Formatting** check box.

5 Click **OK.**

Word will remember your selection and will not track formatting changes in the future.

How do I stop tracking changes?

If you receive comments back from reviewers, you can turn off track changes to stop tracking your text additions, deletions, modifications and your formatting changes.

To turn off track changes:

1   Select the **Review** tab.
    —OR—
    Press **Alt+R**.

2   Click the arrow for the **Track Changes** button in the **Tracking** group.

3   Select **Change Tracking Options**.
    The Track Changes Options dialog box appears.

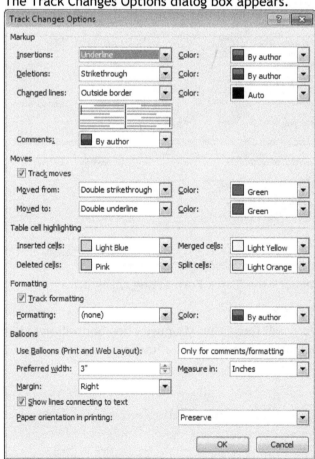

4 In the **Formatting** section, clear the **Track Formatting** check box.

5 Click **OK**.

How do I add a signature line?

You can add a signature line to allow users to sign your printed documents.

To add a signature line:

1 Position your cursor where you want to add the signature.

2 Select the **Insert** tab.
—OR—
Press **Alt+N**.

3 Click the **Signature Line** button in the **Text** group box.

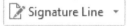

4 Type the signer's name, title, and address.

5 Type any instructions for the signer.

6 Click **OK**.

How do I digitally sign a document?

A digital signature confirms that the information originated from the signer and has not been altered. You can set up an account with a digital signature service to digitally sign documents.

To install a digital signature service:

1 Select the **Insert** tab.
—OR—
Press **Alt+N**.

2 Click the arrow in the lower-right corner of the **Signature Line** button in the **Text** group box.

3 Select **Add Signature Services.**

4 Select and install a signature service.

To digitally sign a document:

1 Position your cursor where you want to add the signature.

2 Select the **Insert** tab.
—OR—
Press **Alt+N.**

3 Click the **Signature Line** button in the **Text** group box.

The Signatures pane appears.

4 Double-click your signature.
The signature is inserted into your document.

How do I compare versions of a document?

You can compare two versions of a document to review any formatting or content changes.

To compare versions:

1 Select the **Review** tab.
—OR—
Press **Alt+R.**

2 Click the **Compare** button in the **Compare** group.

3 Select **Compare**.

The Compare Document dialog box appears.

4 In the **Original document** field, select the original document.

5 In the **Revised document** field, select the document in which you made changes.

6 Click **More** to view more comparison settings.

7 In the **Comparison settings** section, select the types of content you want to compare.

8 Select how you want to **Show changes**.

9 Click **OK**.

The comparison results will appear.

How do I compare two documents side by side?

If you have a wide monitor, you can compare two documents by opening them side-by-side.

To compare two documents side by side:

1 Open the documents that you want to compare.

2 Select the **View** tab.
—OR—
Press **Alt+W**.

3 Click the **View Side by Side** button in the **Window** group.

4 Click the **Arrange All** button in the **Window** group.

5 If you want to scroll through both documents at the same time, click the **Synchronous Scrolling** button in the **Window** group.

How do I print tracked changes and change lines?

If you have tracked changes, you can print the changes and change lines.

To print tracked changes and change lines:

1 Select **File** > **Print**.
—OR—
Press **Ctrl+P**.

2 Click **Settings**.

3 Select **List of Markup**.

4 Click **Print**.

How do I add line numbers?

If you need to distribute Word documents for review, you can add line numbers for reviewers. For example, a reviewer's comment could refer to "line 23" rather than "the 3rd line of the 2nd paragraph."

To add line numbers:

1   Select the **Page Layout** tab.
    —OR—
    Press **Alt+P**.

2   Click the **Line Numbers** button in the **Page Layout** group.

    ¹₂³☐ Line Numbers ▾

3   Select one of the following options:

    ☐   **None** — turn off line numbering for a section where line numbering has been applied.

    ☐   **Continuous** — turn on line numbering for the whole document.

    ☐   **Restart Each Page** — restart line numbering after each page break.

    ☐   **Restart Each Section** — restart line numbering after each section break.

    ☐   **Suppress for Current Paragraph** — turns off line numbering for the current paragraph.

To set advanced line numbering options:

1   Click the **Line Numbers** button in the **Page Layout** group.

    ¹₂³☐ Line Numbers ▾

2 Click **Line Numbering Options.**

The Page Layout dialog box appears.

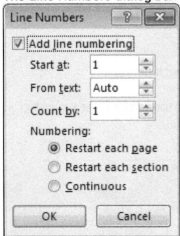

3 Click **Line Numbers.**

The Line Numbers dialog box appears.

4 Set the following options:

- **Start at** — the first line number.

- **From text** — the space between the line number and the content (if the space is too large, some printers may have difficulty printing the numbers and you may not see the numbers on the screen).

- **Count by** — select 1 to display numbers for each line, 2 to display numbers for every other line.

- **Numbering** — select whether to restart line numbering after each page, after each section, or to use continuous line numbers.

5 Click **OK** to close the Line Numbers dialog box.

6 Click **OK** to close the Page Setup dialog box.

How do I count the number of characters or words in a document?

You can use the Word Count feature to count the number of characters, words, lines, paragraphs, and pages in a document or part of a document.

To count the number of characters or words:

1 Select the **Review** tab.
—OR—
Press **Alt+R**.

2 If you want to count part of the document, highlight the content (such as a chapter or paragraph).

3 Click the **Word Count** button in the **Proofing** group.

The Word Count dialog box appears.

How do I print the document properties?

You can include a summary of your document's properties when you print, including the document's path and file name, title, subject, author, and number of pages.

To print the document properties:

1 Select **File** > **Options**.
 The Word Options dialog box appears.

2 Select the **Display** tab.

3 Scroll down to the **Printing options** section.

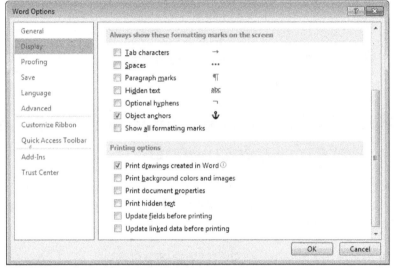

4 Select **Print document properties**.

5 Click **OK**.

User interface (UI)

What are the different areas in the UI?

The Word user interface (UI) include a Quick Access toolbar (QAT), a title bar, tabs, a ribbon, and a status bar.

How do I add a button to the Quick Access Toolbar?

You can add commonly-used features to the Quick Access toolbar (QAT). The QAT appears in Word's title bar above the tabs:

To add a button to the Quick Access Toolbar:

1   Select **File** > **Options**.
    The Word Options dialog box appears.

2 Select Quick Access Toolbar.

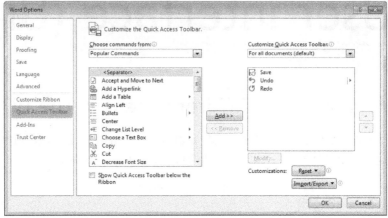

3 Select a command and click **Add**.
The command is added to the Quick Access Toolbar.

4 Click **OK**.

How do I backup or share my Quick Access Toolbar?

If you customize the Quick Access Toolbar (QAT), you should save it to a backup file. If you use more than one computer or plan to upgrade in the future, you can use your backup file to install your QAT on the other computer.

To backup your Quick Access Toolbar:

1 In Windows, navigate to **C:\Users\YourWindowsUserName\ AppData\Local\Microsoft\Office**.

2 Right-click the file named **Word.qat** and select **Copy**.

3 Open the folder on your computer where you want to store the backup.

4 Right-click inside the folder and select **Paste**.

How do I expand or collapse headings? NEW!

If you use heading styles in your document, you can expand or collapse content between two headings. For example, you could collapse all of the chapters in a document except chapter 2. If you send the document to another user, they will only see chapter 2 unless they expand the other chapters.

◇ *All of the content is visible in Draft or Outline view.*

To expand or collapse a heading:

1 Hover over a heading.
   An arrow will appear to the left of the heading.

2 Click the arrow.

To expand or collapse all headings:

1 Right-click any heading.

2 Select **Expand/Collapse** > **Expand All Headings** or **Collapse All Headings**.

How do I close Word's panes without using the mouse?

You can use keyboard shortcuts to close the panes that open on the left and right side of the main window. For example, you can close the Navigation pane or the Styles pane if you are not using it.

To close a pane:

1 Press **F6** to move the focus to the pane.

2 Press **Ctrl+Space** to open the pane's popup menu.

3 Press **C** to close the pane.

How do I turn on gridlines?

You can use gridlines to align content in a document such as paragraphs, pictures, WordArt, graphs, or charts.

To turn on gridlines:

1 Select the **View** tab.
   —OR—
   Press **Alt+W**.

2 Select the **Gridlines** check box in the **Show** group.

My content disappears when I type!

If content disappears when you type, you are probably in overwrite mode.

To turn off overwrite mode:

1 Select **File** > **Options**.
   The Word Options dialog box appears.

2 Click the **Advanced** tab.

3 Scroll to the **Editing options** section.

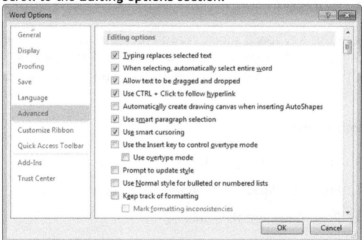

4   Clear the **Use overtype mode** check box.

5   Click **OK**.

How do I hide the "extra" space between pages?

In Print Layout view, a small amount of space appears between pages to make the page breaks more visible.

This extra space is often helpful, but it can be annoying on small monitors or when you need to view the bottom of the previous page and the top of the current page at the same time.

To hide the space between pages in Print Layout view:

1   Select **File** > **Options**.
The Word Options dialog box appears.

2   Select the **Display** tab.

3   Scroll to the **Page Display options** section.

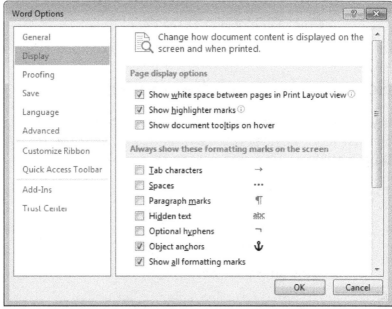

4   Uncheck the **Show white space between pages in Print Layout view** check box.

5   Click **OK**.

How do I view thumbnails of my pages?

You can use the Navigation pane to view small images ("thumbnails") of the pages n your document.

To view page thumbnails:

1   If the Navigation Pane is not currently open:
Select the **View** tab.
Select the **Navigation Pane** checkbox in the **Show** group.

2   Click the [⊞] **Browse the pages in your document**.
The page thumbnails appear.

To enlarge the thumbnails:

1   Click the border on the right side of the Navigation Pane.
The mouse pointer should change to a double-sided arrow.

2   Drag the mouse pointer to the right.

How do I turn off drag-and-drop?

If you use a trackpad, don't like to use the mouse, or are using another input device, you may want to turn off the Drag and Drop feature.

To turn off drag and drop:

1   Select **File** > **Options**.
The Word Options dialog box appears.

2   Click the **Advanced** tab.

3 Scroll to the **Editing options** section.

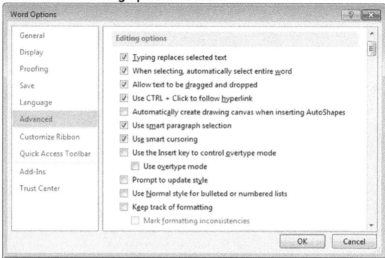

4 Uncheck **Allow text to be dragged and dropped.**

5 Click **OK.**

How do I hide the mini toolbar when I select text?

By default, Word display a small toolbar when you select text:

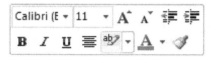

You can hide the mini formatting toolbar if you find it distracting.

To hide the mini toolbar:

1 Select **File > Options.**
The Word Options dialog box appears.

2   Select the **General** tab.

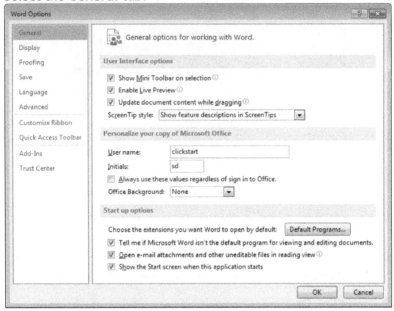

3   Clear the **Show Mini Toolbar on selection** check box.

4   Click **OK**.

How do I hide the vertical scrollbar?

You can use the vertical scrollbar on the right side of the Word window to scroll through your document. If you use the Page Up and Page Down keys instead of the scrollbar, you can hide the scrollbar to save screen space.

To hide the vertical scrollbar:

1   Select **File** > **Options**.
The Word Options dialog box appears.

2   Select the **Advanced** tab.

3 Scroll down to the **Display** section.

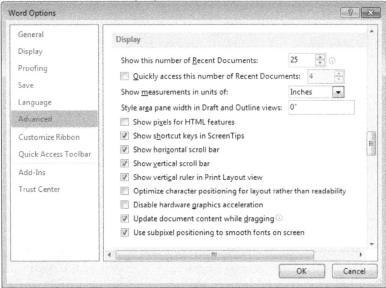

4 Uncheck **Show vertical scroll bar.**

5 Click **OK.**

How do I minimize Word?

You can press **Windows+M** to minimize all of your open applications, including Word.

The Windows key looks like the Windows logo: ⊞.

How do I split the window?

If you want to copy or move items between parts of a long document, it can be useful to split the document window into two panes. This allows you to display the item you want to copy or move in one pane and the destination for the item in the other pane.

To split a window:

1 Select the **View** tab.
—OR—
Press **Alt+W**.

2 Click the **Split** button in the **Window** group.

The grey split bar appears.

3 Position the cursor where you want to split the screen.

4 Click to place the split bar.

To copy or move an item from one pane to another, you can use the Cut, Copy, and Paste commands, or you can drag the item between the panes.

When you are finished editing the document:

☐ Double-click the split bar to restore the window to a single pane.
—OR—
Select the **View** tab and click the **Remove Split** button in the **Window** group.

How do I turn on audible feedback?

You can turn on audible feedback to hear a sound when panes, comments, or error messages appear. Audible feedback could be useful for users who have trouble seeing or if you enjoy hearing the sounds.

To turn on audible feedback:

1 Select **File > Options**.
The Word Options dialog box appears.

2 Select the **Advanced** tab.

3 Scroll down to the **General** section.

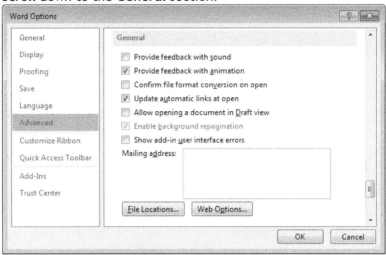

4 Select the **Provide Feedback with Sound** option.

5 Click **OK**.

How do I add a screen tip?

You can use bookmarks to add screen tips to a word or phrase in a document. For example, you could use screen tips to add instructions, definitions, or other useful information for your reviewers or readers. The content with a screen tip will appear as a link. When the reader clicks the link, the screen tip appears in a pop-up window.

To add a screen tip:

1 Select the text to be hyperlinked.

2 Select the **Insert** tab.
—OR—
Press **Alt+N**.

3 Click the **Bookmark** button in the **Links** group.

The Bookmark dialog box appears.

4 Type a **Bookmark name**.

5 Click **Add**.

6 While the text is still selected, press **Ctrl+K**.
The Insert Hyperlink dialog box appears.

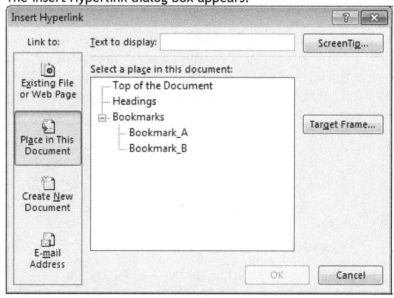

7 Click **ScreenTip**.
The Set Hyperlink ScreenTip dialog box appears.

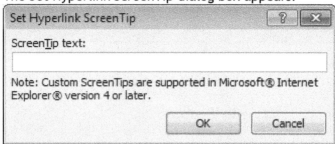

8 Type the text you want to use for your screen tip.

9 Click **OK**.

10 Click **Place in This Document**.
A list of locations appears.

11 In the list of locations, select the name of the bookmark you created in step 3.

12 Click **OK**.

When you're finished, you will have a link that goes nowhere. If you hover over the link, a popup screen tip will appear with your message. If you click the link, the cursor will move to the beginning of the bookmark.

How do I show or hide the rulers?

You can show the ruler to set up tabs and hanging indents.

To show or hide the ruler:

1 Select the **View** tab.
—OR—
Press **Alt+W**.

2 Select the **Ruler** checkbox in the **Show** group.

How do I measure distances with the ruler?

The ruler is useful for setting tabs and margins. You can use the ruler to view the distance between tabs and to measure their distance from the left and right sides of the page.

To measure distances with the ruler:

1   Click a tab or margin marker on the ruler.

2   While still holding the left mouse button, press the right mouse button.

3   Slightly move the mouse.
    The distance measurements appear.

How do I count the words in a document?

Word displays the current page count and word count in the status bar at the bottom left of the window. You can insert the word count into a document, if needed.

To insert the word count:

1   Position the insertion point where you want to insert the word count.

2   Select the **Insert** tab.
    —OR—
    Press **Alt+N**.

3   Click the **Quick Parts** button in the **Text** group.

4   Select **Field**.

The Field dialog box appears.

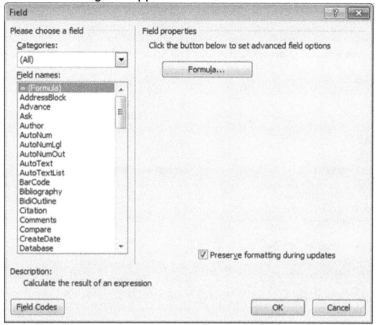

5   In the **Categories** list, select **Document Information**.

6   Select **NumWords** from the **Field Names** list.

7   Click **OK**.

How do I show or hide formatting markers?

You can show or hide formatting markers such as spaces, paragraph marks, and tabs. Viewing the formatting markers may be distracting at first, but they're useful if you need to troubleshoot formatting issues.

To show or hide the formatting markers:

1   Select the **Home** tab.
—OR—
Press **Alt+H**.

2   Click the ¶ **Show/Hide** button in the **Paragraph** group.

TIP▶ *You can also press **Ctrl+Shift+*** (asterisk) to show or hide formatting markers.*

When you press or add...	The character or content will appear as...
Space	▪
Enter	¶ (paragraph mark)
Tab	→
Hidden text	Underlined with dots
Optional hyphen (inserted by pressing **Ctrl+Hyphen**)	¬
Non-breaking hyphen (inserted by pressing **Ctrl+Shift+Hyphen**)	-
Non-breaking space (inserted by pressing **Ctrl+Shift+Space**)	

How do I open the help system?

Word includes an extensive help system, including step-by-step instructions, training videos, tips for using Word on a tablet, and links to Web sites about Word.

To open the help system:

- ☐ Click the ? **Help** icon in the far right of the title bar.

Keyboard shortcuts

How do I repeat an action?

If you want to repeat an action, such as applying a style, inserting a table, or creating a list, press **F4** or **Crl+Y**.

How do I print a list of keyboard shortcuts?

You can assign a keyboard shortcut to a macro, style, or built-in Word command. You can also print a list of the built-in and user-assigned keyboard shortcuts.

To print a list of keyboard shortcuts:

1 Select **File** > **Print**.
   —OR—
   Press **Ctrl+P**.

2 Click **Settings** and select **Key Assignments**.

3 Click **Print**.

How do I view keyboard shortcuts?

You can press Alt to see the shortcut Alt shortcut key shortcuts for the tabs in the ribbon and the buttons in the Quick Access Toolbar:

Shortcut	Result
Alt+H	Open the Home tab
Alt+N	Open the Insert tab
Alt+D	Open the Design tab

Shortcut	Result
Alt+P	Open the Page Layout tab
Alt+S	Open the Reference tab
Alt+M	Open the Merge tab
Alt+R	Open the Review tab
Alt+W	Open the View tab
Alt+L	Open the Developer tab
Alt+C	Open the Mathematics tab
Alt+1	Activate the first button in the Quick Access Toolbar
Alt+2	Activate the second button in the Quick Access Toolbar
Alt+3	Activate the third button in the Quick Access Toolbar

Keyboard shortcuts (by key)

Shortcut	Result
/ (slash) on the numeric keypad	Hide or display character formatting
Alt	View Alt key shortcuts for tabs in the ribbon
Alt+highlight	Vertically select content
Alt+↓ (down arrow)	Open a selected drop-down list
Alt+← (left arrow)	Go back one page
Alt+→ (right arrow)	Go forward one page
Alt+5 on the keypad (with Num Lock off)	Select an entire table
Alt+End	Move to the last cell in a row
Alt+F3	When text or an object is selected, open the Create New Building Block dialog box
Alt+F5	Restore the size of the active window after you maximize it
Alt+F9	Switch between all field codes and their results

Shortcut	Result
Alt+Home	Move to the first cell in a row
Alt+Page Down	Move to the last cell in a column
Alt+Page Up	Move to the first cell in a column
Alt+PrntScr	Copy a picture of the selected window to the clipboard
Alt+Tab	Switch to the next window
Alt+Ctrl+- (minus sign)	Insert an em (—) dash
Alt+Ctrl+. (period)	Insert an ellipsis
Alt+Ctrl+Page Down	Move to the end of the window
Alt+Ctrl+Page Up	Move to the top of the window
Alt+Ctrl+1	Apply the Heading 1 style
Alt+Ctrl+2	Apply the Heading 2 style
Alt+Ctrl+3	Apply the Heading 3 style
Alt+Ctrl+C	Insert the copyright symbol
Alt+Ctrl+D	Insert an endnote
Alt+Ctrl+F	Insert a footnote
Alt+Ctrl+I	Switch to print preview
Alt+Ctrl+K	Start AutoFormat
Alt+Ctrl+L	Insert a ListNum field
Alt+Ctrl+M	Insert a comment
Alt+Ctrl+N	Switch to Draft view
Alt+Ctrl+O	Switch to Outline view
Alt+Ctrl+P	Switch to Print Layout view
Alt+Ctrl+R	Insert the registered trademark symbol
Alt+Ctrl+S	Split the document window
Alt+Ctrl+T	Insert the trademark symbol
Alt+Ctrl+Y	Repeat find (after closing Find and Replace window)
Alt+Ctrl+Z	Move between the last four places you've edited

Shortcut	Result
Alt+Shift+- (minus sign)	Collapse text under a heading
Alt+Shift+↓ (down arrow)	Move selected paragraph(s) down or move one row down in a table
Alt+Shift+← (left arrow)	Promote a paragraph
Alt+Shift+→ (right arrow)	Demote a paragraph
Alt+Shift+↑ (up arrow)	Move selected paragraph(s) up
Alt+Shift+↑ (up arrow)	Move one row up
Alt+Shift++ (plus sign)	Expand text under a heading
Alt+Shift+1	Show all headings with the Heading 1 style
Alt+Shift+A	Expand or collapse all
Alt+Shift+C	Close the Reviewing Pane if it is open
Alt+Shift+D	Insert a Date field
Alt+Shift+E	Edit a mail-merge data document
Alt+Shift+F	Insert a Merge field
Alt+Shift+I	Mark a table of authorities entry (citation)
Alt+Shift+K	Preview a mail merge
Alt+Shift+L	Show the first line of body text or all body text
Alt+Shift+M	Print the merged document
Alt+Shift+N	Merge a document
Alt+Shift+n	Show all headings up to Heading n
Alt+Shift+O	Mark a table of contents entry
Alt+Shift+P	Insert a Page field
Alt+Shift+R	Copy the header or footer used in the previous section of the document
Alt+Shift+S	Remove the document window split
Alt+Shift+T	Insert a Time field
Alt+Shift+Tab	Switch to the previous window
Alt+Shift+X	Mark an index entry
Alt+Ctrl+Shift+Page Down	Extend a selection to the end of a window
Alt+Ctrl+Shift+S	Open Styles task pane

Shortcut	Result
Ctrl+F1	Expand or collapse the ribbon
Ctrl+F3	Cut to the spike
Ctrl+F4	Close the active window
Ctrl+F6	When more than one window is open, switch to the next window
Ctrl+F9	Insert an empty field
Ctrl+F10	Maximize or restore a selected window
Ctrl+F11	Lock a field
Ctrl+- (minus sign)	Insert an en (-) dash
Ctrl+↓ (down arrow)	Move one paragraph down
Ctrl+← (left arrow)	Move one word to the left
Ctrl+→ (right arrow)	Move one word to the right
Ctrl+↑ (up arrow)	Move one paragraph up
Ctrl+Backspace	Delete one word to the left
Ctrl+[	Decrease font size 1 point
Ctrl+]	Increase font size 1 point
Ctrl+]	Increase font size 1 point
Ctrl+= (equal sign)	Apply subscript formatting (automatic spacing)
Ctrl+Delete	Delete one word to the right
Ctrl+End	Move to the end of the document or last preview page when zoomed out
Ctrl+Enter	Insert a page break
Ctrl+Home	Move to the beginning of a document or the first preview page when zoomed out
Ctrl+Hyphen	Insert an optional hyphen
Ctrl+Page Down	Move to the top of the next page
Ctrl+Page Up	Move to the top of the previous page
Ctrl+Space	Remove paragraph or character formatting
Ctrl+Tab	Switch to the next tab in a dialog box

Shortcut	Result
Ctrl+0 (zero)	Add or remove one line space preceding a paragraph
Ctrl+1	Set single spacing
Ctrl+2	Set double spacing
Ctrl+5	Set 1.5 line spacing
Ctrl+A	Select entire document
Ctrl+B	Boldface content
Ctrl+C	Copy the selected text or object
Ctrl+D	Open the Font dialog box to change the formatting of characters
Ctrl+E	Switch a paragraph between centered and left-aligned
Ctrl+F	Open the Navigation task pane to find content
Ctrl+G	Open the Go To dialog box
Ctrl+H	Open the Find and Replace dialog box
Ctrl+I	Italicize content
Ctrl+J	Switch a paragraph between justified and left-aligned
Ctrl+K	Insert a hyperlink
Ctrl+L	Left align a paragraph
Ctrl+M	Indent a paragraph from the left
Ctrl+N	Create a new document
Ctrl+O	Open a document
Ctrl+P	Print a document
Ctrl+Q	Remove paragraph formatting
Ctrl+R	Switch a paragraph between right-aligned and left-aligned
Ctrl+S	Save a document
Ctrl+Alt+V	Open the paste special options
Ctrl+Shift+F3	Paste the spike contents
Ctrl+Shift+F6	Switch to the previous window

Shortcut	Result
Ctrl+Shift+F7	Update linked information
Ctrl+Shift+F8, then arrow keys	Select a vertical block of text (press ESC to cancel)
Ctrl+Shift+F9	Unlink a field
Ctrl+Shift+F11	Unlock a field
Ctrl+Shift+↓ (down arrow)	Extend a selection to the end of a paragraph
Ctrl+Shift+← (left arrow)	Extend a selection to the beginning of a word
Ctrl+Shift+→ (right arrow)	Extend a selection to the end of a word
Ctrl+Shift+↑ (up arrow)	Extend a selection to the beginning of a paragraph
Ctrl+Shift+*	Display non-printing characters

◇ *Asterisk on numeric keypad does not work.* |
Ctrl+Shift++ (plus sign)	Apply superscript formatting (automatic spacing)
Ctrl+Shift+<	Decrease font size one point
Ctrl+Shift+>	Increase font size one point
Ctrl+Shift+End	Extend a selection to the end of a document
Ctrl+Shift+Enter	Insert a column break
Ctrl+Shift+Home	Extend a selection to the beginning of a document
Ctrl+Shift+Hyphen	Insert a non-breaking hyphen
Ctrl+Shift+Space	Insert a non-breaking space
Ctrl+Shift+Tab	Switch to the previous tab in a dialog box
Ctrl+Shift+A	Format all letters as capitals
Ctrl+Shift+C	Copy formatting
Ctrl+Shift+D	Double-underline text
Ctrl+Shift+E	Turn change tracking on or off
Ctrl+Shift+F	Open the Font dialog box
Ctrl+Shift+G	Open the Word Count dialog box

Shortcut	Result
Ctrl+Shift+H	Apply hidden text formatting
Ctrl+Shift+K	Format letters as small capitals
Ctrl+Shift+M	Remove a paragraph indent from the left
Ctrl+Shift+N	Apply the Normal style or demote to body text in Outline view
Ctrl+Shift+Q	Change the selection to the Symbol font
Ctrl+Shift+S	Open Apply Styles task pane
Ctrl+Shift+T	Reduce a hanging indent
Ctrl+Shift+V	Apply copied formatting to text
Ctrl+Shift+W	Underline words but not spaces
Ctrl+Shift+Z	Extend a selection to the end of a page
Ctrl+T	Create a hanging indent
Ctrl+U	Underline content
Ctrl+V	Paste text or an object
Ctrl+W	Close a document or the active window
Ctrl+X	Cut the selected text or object
Ctrl+Y	Redo or repeat an action
Ctrl+Z	Undo the last action
F1	Get help on the selected item
	If no Help topic is associated with the selected item, a general Help topic appears.
F2, move the cursor, press Enter	Move content
F6	Move the focus to select each of the following areas of the window:
	☐ Active ribbon tab
	☐ Task panes
	☐ Status bar
	☐ Document
F6	Move to a task pane from another pane (clockwise direction)

Shortcut	Result
F8	Press once to select a word, twice to select a sentence, three times to select a cell or paragraph, and four times to select all
F8, then Left Arrow or Right Arrow	Select the nearest character
F9	Update selected fields
F10	View Alt key shortcuts for tabs in the ribbon
F11	Go to the next field
Backspace	Delete one character to the left
Delete	Delete one character to the right
End	Move to the end of a line
Esc	Cancel an action
Home	Move to the beginning of a line
Page Down	Move down one screen or preview page when zoomed out
Page Up	Move up one screen or preview page when zoomed out
PrntScr	Copy a picture of the screen to the clipboard
Shift+F1, click any text	Review text formatting
Shift+F2, move the cursor, press Enter	Copy content
Shift+F3	Change the case of letters
Shift+F5	Move to a previous revision or last location when the document was last closed
Shift+F6	Move to a task pane from another pane (counter-clockwise direction)
Shift+F8	Reduce the size of a selection
Shift+F9	Switch between a selected field code and its result
Shift+F10	Open a menu or, when a building block is selected, display its shortcut menu
Shift+F11	Go to the previous field
Shift+↓ (down arrow)	Extend a selection one line down

Shortcut	Result
Shift+← (left arrow)	Extend a selection one character to the left
Shift+→ (right arrow)	Extend a selection one character to the right
Shift+↑ (up arrow)	Extend a selection one line up
Shift+End	Extend a selection to the end of a line
Shift+Enter	Insert a line break
Shift+Home	Extend a selection to the beginning of a line
Shift+Page Down	Extend a selection one screen down
Shift+Page Up	Extend a selection one screen up
Shift+Tab	Move to the previous option, option group, or cell in a table
Space or Enter	Activate the selected item
Tab	Move to the next command, option, option group, or cell in a table

Common tasks

Shortcut	Result
Ctrl+Space	Remove paragraph or character formatting
Ctrl+[	Decrease font size 1 point
Ctrl+]	Increase font size 1 point
Ctrl+B	Boldface content
Ctrl+C	Copy the selected text or object
Ctrl+I	Italicize content
Ctrl+U	Underline content
Ctrl+V	Paste text or an object
Ctrl+X	Cut the selected text or object
Ctrl+Alt+V	Open the paste special options
Ctrl+Shift+Space	Insert a non-breaking space

Shortcut	Result
Ctrl+Shift+Hyphen	Insert a non-breaking hyphen
Ctrl+Shift+<	Decrease font size one value
Ctrl+Shift+>	Increase font size one value
Ctrl+Shift+G	Open the Word Count dialog box
Ctrl+Shift+V	Paste the formatting only

Align paragraphs

Shortcut	Result
Alt+Ctrl+1	Apply the Heading 1 style
Alt+Ctrl+2	Apply the Heading 2 style
Alt+Ctrl+3	Apply the Heading 3 style
Alt+Ctrl+K	Start AutoFormat
Alt+Ctrl+Shift+S	Open Styles task pane
Ctrl+Shift+N	Apply the Normal style
Ctrl+Shift+S	Open Apply Styles task pane

Change or resize font

Shortcut	Result
Ctrl+]	Increase the font size by 1 point
Ctrl+[	Decrease the font size by 1 point
Ctrl+Shift+>	Increase the font size
Ctrl+Shift+<	Decrease the font size
Ctrl+Shift+F	Open the Font dialog box

Character formatting

Shortcut	Result
Ctrl+Space	Remove manual character formatting
Ctrl+Equal Sign	Apply subscript formatting (automatic spacing)
Ctrl+Shift+Plus Sign	Apply superscript formatting (automatic spacing)
Ctrl+B	Apply bold formatting
Ctrl+D	Open the Font dialog box to change the formatting of characters
Ctrl+I	Apply italic formatting
Ctrl+U	Apply an underline
Ctrl+Shift+A	Format all letters as capitals
Ctrl+Shift+D	Double-underline text
Ctrl+Shift+H	Apply hidden text formatting
Ctrl+Shift+K	Format letters as small capitals
Ctrl+Shift+W	Underline words but not spaces
Ctrl+Shift+Q	Change the selection to the Symbol font
Shift+F3	Change the case of letters

Copy and paste

Shortcut	Result
F2, move the cursor, press Enter	Move content
Shift+F2, move the cursor, press Enter	Copy content
Alt+F3	When text or an object is selected, open the Create New Building Block dialog box
Alt+Shift+R	Copy the header or footer used in the previous section of the document
Ctrl+F3	Cut to the spike

Shortcut	Result
Ctrl+C	Copy selected content to the clipboard
Ctrl+X	Cut selected content to the clipboard
Ctrl+V	Paste from the clipboard
Ctrl+Shift+F3	Paste the spike contents
Shift+F10	When a building block is selected, display its shortcut menu

Copy formatting

Shortcut	Result
Ctrl+Shift+C	Copy formatting from text
Ctrl+Shift+V	Apply copied formatting to text

Create, view, and save

Shortcut	Result
Alt+Ctrl+S	Split the document window
Alt+Shift+S	Remove the document window split
Ctrl+N	Create a new document
Ctrl+O	Open a document
Ctrl+S	Save a document
Ctrl+W	Close a document

Delete content

Shortcut	Result
Backspace	Delete one character to the left

Shortcut	Result
Delete	Delete one character to the right
Ctrl+F3	Cut to the spike
Ctrl+Backspace	Delete one word to the left
Ctrl+Delete	Delete one word to the right
Ctrl+X	Cut selected text to the clipboard
Ctrl+Z	Undo the last action

Extend a selection

Shortcut	Result
F8	Press once to select a word, twice to select a sentence, three times to select a cell or paragraph, and four times to select all
F8, then Left Arrow or Right Arrow	Select the nearest character
Shift+F8	Reduce the size of a selection
Esc	Turn extend mode off
Alt+highlight	Vertically select content
Alt+Ctrl+Shift+Page Down	Extend a selection to the end of a window
Ctrl+Shift+Left Arrow	Extend a selection to the beginning of a word
Ctrl+Shift+Right Arrow	Extend a selection to the end of a word
Shift+Up Arrow	Extend a selection one line up
Shift+Down Arrow	Extend a selection one line down
Shift+Left Arrow	Extend a selection one character to the left
Shift+Right Arrow	Extend a selection one character to the right
Shift+Home	Extend a selection to the beginning of a line
Shift+End	Extend a selection to the end of a line

Shortcut	Result
Shift+Page Up	Extend a selection one screen up
Shift+Page Down	Extend a selection one screen down
Ctrl+A	Select entire document
Ctrl+Shift+F8, then arrow keys	Select a vertical block of text (press ESC to cancel)
Ctrl+Shift+Home	Extend a selection to the beginning of a document
Ctrl+Shift+End	Extend a selection to the end of a document
Ctrl+Shift+Up Arrow	Extend a selection to the beginning of a paragraph
Ctrl+Shift+Down Arrow	Extend a selection to the end of a paragraph
Ctrl+Shift+Z	Extend a selection to the end of a page

Fields

Shortcut	Result
Alt+Shift+D	Insert a Date field
Alt+Shift+P	Insert a Page field
Alt+Shift+T	Insert a Time field
Alt+Ctrl+L	Insert a ListNum field
Ctrl+F9	Insert an empty field
Ctrl+F11	Lock a field
Ctrl+Shift+F7	Update linked information
Ctrl+Shift+F9	Unlink a field
Alt+F9	Switch between all field codes and their results
Shift+F9	Switch between a selected field code and its result
Shift+F11	Go to the previous field
Ctrl+Shift+F11	Unlock a field
F9	Update selected fields

Shortcut	Result
F11	Go to the next field

Find, replace, and browse

Shortcut	Result
Alt+Ctrl+Y	Repeat find (after closing Find and Replace window)
Alt+Ctrl+Z	Move between the last four places you've edited
Ctrl+F	Open the Navigation task pane to find content
Ctrl+G	Open the Go To dialog box
Ctrl+H	Open the Find and Replace dialog box

Formatting

Shortcut	Result
Ctrl+Shift+*	Display non-printing characters ◇ *Asterisk on numeric keypad does not work.*
Ctrl+Shift+C	Copy formats
Ctrl+Shift+V	Paste formats
Shift+F1, click any text	Review text formatting

Keyboard

Shortcut	Result
Alt or F10	View Alt key shortcuts for tabs in the ribbon
F1	Get help on the selected item

Shortcut	Result
	If no Help topic is associated with the selected item, a general Help topic appears.
F6	Move the focus to select each of the following areas of the window:
	□ Active ribbon tab
	□ Task panes
	□ Status bar
	□ Document
Tab or Shift+Tab	Move the focus to each command on the ribbon
Up Arrow, Down Arrow, Left Arrow, or Right Arrow	Move up, down, left, or right between items in the ribbon
Space or Enter	Activate the selected item
Tab	Move to the next option or option group
Ctrl+Tab	Switch to the next tab in a dialog box
Shift+Tab	Move to the previous option or option group
Ctrl+F1	Expand or collapse the Ribbon
Ctrl+Space	Display the full set of commands on the task pane menu
Ctrl+Tab	When a menu is active, move to a task pane. (You may need to press Ctrl+Tab more than once.)
Ctrl+Shift+Tab	Switch to the previous tab in a dialog box
Shift+F10	Open a menu
Home or End	Select the first or last item in a gallery
Page Up or Page Down	Scroll up or down in the selected gallery list
Esc	Close a selected drop-down list or cancel a command and close a dialog box
Arrow keys	Move between options in a drop-down list or group of options
First letter of an option in a drop-down list	Select an option from a drop-down list

Shortcut	Result
PrntScr	Copy a picture of the screen to the clipboard
Alt+PrntScr	Copy a picture of the selected window to the clipboard
Alt+Down Arrow	Open a selected drop-down list
Alt+underlined letter in an option	Select an option or select/clear a check box
Alt+Tab	Switch to the next window
Alt+Shift+Tab	Switch to the previous window
Alt+F5	Restore the size of the active window after you maximize it
F6	Move to a task pane from another pane (clockwise direction)
Ctrl+F6	When more than one window is open, switch to the next window
Shift+F6	Move to a task pane from another pane (counter-clockwise direction)
Ctrl+Shift+F6	Switch to the previous window
Ctrl+W or Ctrl+F4	Close the active window
Ctrl+F10	Maximize or restore a selected window

Line spacing

Shortcut	Result
Ctrl+0 (zero)	Add or remove one line space preceding a paragraph
Ctrl+1	Set single spacing
Ctrl+2	Set double spacing
Ctrl+5	Set 1.5 line spacing

Mail merge

Shortcut	Result
Alt+Shift+E	Edit a mail-merge data document
Alt+Shift+F	Insert a merge field
Alt+Shift+K	Preview a mail merge
Alt+Shift+M	Print the merged document
Alt+Shift+N	Merge a document

Navigate a document

Shortcut	Result
Home	Move to the beginning of a line
End	Move to the end of a line
Page Up	Move up one screen
Page Down	Move down one screen
Up Arrow	Move up one line
Down Arrow	Move down one line
Left Arrow	Move one character to the left
Right Arrow	Move one character to the right
Alt+Ctrl+Page Up	Move to the top of the window
Alt+Ctrl+Page Down	Move to the end of the window
Ctrl+Home	Move to the beginning of a document
Ctrl+End	Move to the end of the document
Ctrl+Page Up	Move to the top of the previous page
Ctrl+Page Down	Move to the top of the next page
Ctrl+Up Arrow	Move one paragraph up
Ctrl+Down Arrow	Move one paragraph down

Shortcut	Result
Ctrl+Left Arrow	Move one word to the left
Ctrl+Right Arrow	Move one word to the right
Shift+F5	Move to a previous revision or last location when the document was last closed

Outline view

Shortcut	Result
Alt+Shift+Up Arrow	Move selected paragraph(s) up
Alt+Shift+Down Arrow	Move selected paragraph(s) down
Alt+Shift+Left Arrow	Promote a paragraph
Alt+Shift+Right Arrow	Demote a paragraph
Alt+Shift+Plus Sign	Expand text under a heading
Alt+Shift+Minus Sign	Collapse text under a heading
Alt+Shift+1	Show all headings with the Heading 1 style
Alt+Shift+*n*	Show all headings up to Heading n
Alt+Shift+A	Expand or collapse all
Alt+Shift+L	Show the first line of body text or all body text
Ctrl+Tab	Insert a tab
Ctrl+Shift+N	Demote to body text
Slash (/) on the numeric keypad	Hide or display character formatting

Paragraph styles

Shortcut	Result
Ctrl+E	Switch a paragraph between centered and left-aligned

Shortcut	Result
Ctrl+J	Switch a paragraph between justified and left-aligned
Ctrl+L	Left align a paragraph
Ctrl+M	Indent a paragraph from the left
Ctrl+Q	Remove paragraph formatting
Ctrl+R	Switch a paragraph between right-aligned and left-aligned
Ctrl+T	Create a hanging indent
Ctrl+Shift+M	Remove a paragraph indent from the left
Ctrl+Shift+T	Reduce a hanging indent

Print and preview documents

Shortcut	Result
Arrow keys	Move around the preview page when zoomed in
Page Up or Page Down	Move by one preview page when zoomed out
Alt+Ctrl+I	Switch to print preview
Ctrl+Home	Move to the first preview page when zoomed out
Ctrl+End	Move to the last preview page when zoomed out
Ctrl+P	Print a document

Read mode

Shortcut	Result
Home	Go to beginning of document
End	Go to end of document
Esc	Exit read mode

Shortcut	Result
Any number+Enter	Go to page *n*

References, footnotes, and endnotes

Shortcut	Description
Alt+Ctrl+D	Insert an endnote
Alt+Ctrl+F	Insert a footnote
Alt+Shift+I	Mark a table of authorities entry (citation)
Alt+Shift+O	Mark a table of contents entry
Alt+Shift+X	Mark an index entry

Reviewing documents

Shortcut	Result
Alt+Ctrl+M	Insert a comment
Alt+Shift+C	Close the Reviewing Pane if it is open
Ctrl+Shift+E	Turn change tracking on or off

Special characters

Shortcut	Result
Alt+Ctrl+Minus Sign	Insert an em (—) dash
Alt+Ctrl+. (period)	Insert an ellipsis
Alt+Ctrl+C	Insert the copyright symbol
Alt+Ctrl+R	Insert the registered trademark symbol
Alt+Ctrl+T	Insert the trademark symbol

Shortcut	Result
Ctrl+F9	Insert a field
Ctrl+Enter	Insert a page break
Ctrl+Shift+Enter	Insert a column break
Ctrl+Minus Sign	Insert an en (–) dash
Ctrl+Hyphen	Insert an optional hyphen
Ctrl+Shift+Space	Insert a non-breaking space
Ctrl+Shift+Hyphen	Insert a non-breaking hyphen
Shift+Enter	Insert a line break

Switch view

Shortcut	Result
Alt+Ctrl+N	Switch to Draft view
Alt+Ctrl+O	Switch to Outline view
Alt+Ctrl+P	Switch to Print Layout view

Tables

Shortcut	Result
Tab	Move to the next cell in a row
Up Arrow	Move to the previous row
Down Arrow	Move to the next row
Alt+Home	Move to the first cell in a row
Alt+End	Move to the last cell in a row
Alt+Page Up	Move to the first cell in a column
Alt+Page Down	Move to the last cell in a column

Shortcut	Result
Alt+Shift+Up Arrow	Move one row up
Alt+Shift+Down Arrow	Move one row down
Alt+5 on the keypad (with Num Lock off)	Select an entire table
Ctrl+Tab	Insert a tab
Shift+Tab	Move to the previous cell in a row

Undo and Redo

Shortcut	Result
Esc	Cancel an action
Ctrl+Y	Redo or repeat an action
Ctrl+Z	Undo an action

Web pages

Shortcut	Result
F9	Refresh
Alt+Left Arrow	Go back one page
Alt+Right Arrow	Go forward one page
Ctrl+K	Insert a hyperlink

Index

CSS to the Point

CSS to the Point provides focused answers to over 150 cascading stylesheet (CSS) questions. Each answer includes a description of the solution, a graphical example, and sample code that has been tested in Internet Explorer, Firefox, Chrome, Opera, and Safari. If you have been struggling with CSS, this book will help you use CSS like a pro.

You can order *CSS to the Point* at **www.lulu.com/clickstart**

HTML5 to the Point

HTML5 to the Point provides focused answers to over 140 HTML5 questions. Each answer includes a description of the solution and sample code that you can use in your documents. If you want to learn HTML5, this book will help you use it like a pro.

You can order *HTML5 to the Point* at **www.lulu.com/clickstart**.

MadCap Flare Developer's Guide

With this easy-to-use and comprehensive guide, you can learn how to organize, write, design, and publish online help, user guides, knowledge bases, policies and procedures, and more using the industry benchmark for single source publishing: MadCap Flare. It includes detailed information about importing content from RoboHelp, Word, and FrameMaker and provides step-by-step instructions for using all of Flare's features. If you want to use Flare like a pro, this is your guide.

You can order *MadCap Flare Developer's Guide* at **www.lulu.com/clickstart**.

Training

ClickStart offers training for Microsoft Word, MadCap Flare, Adobe Captivate, HTML5, and CSS. Our Word training classes extend what you have learned in this book with practice exercises, best practices, and advanced challenges.

We teach online and onsite classes (worldwide), and we offer group discounts for 4 or more students. For more information, visit our website at **www.clickstart.net** or email us at **info@clickstart.net**.

Consulting

ClickStart also offers a full range of consulting and contracting services, including:

- Developing technical documentation and training guides
- Developing policies and procedures
- Designing Word templates, themes, styles, and documents
- Single sourcing content for multiple audiences
- Migrating RoboHelp, FrameMaker, and Word projects to Flare
- Developing context-sensitive help and embedded user assistance

For more information, visit our website at **www.clickstart.net** or email us at **info@clickstart.net**.